MW01710233

- Biography Series -

Famous Women

PERSONALITIES

by
Vinita

FIRST EDITION
An imprint of Sura Books (Pvt) Ltd.
(An ISO 9001:2000 Certified Company)
Chennai • Ernakulam
Bengalooru • Thiruvananthapuram

Price: Rs.40.00

S.B. BOOK STALL ADOOR Ph: 227481

©PUBLISHERS

FAMOUS WOMEN PERSONALITIES

BY

Vinita

This Edition : February, 2010

Size : 1/8 Demy

Pages : 96

Code No. : BI 10

Price: Rs.40.00

ISBN: 81-7478-555-6

[NO ONE IS PERMITTED TO COPY OR TRANSLATE IN ANY OTHER LANGUAGE THE CONTENTS OF THIS BOOK OR PART THEREOF IN ANY FORM WITHOUT THE WRITTEN PERMISSION OF THE PUBLISHERS]

FIRST EDITION

[An imprint of Sura Books (Pvt) Ltd.]

Head Office: 1620, 'J' Block, 16th Main Road, Anna Nagar,
Chennai - 600 040. Phones: 044-26162173, 26161099.

Branches :

- XXXII/2328, New Kalavath Road,
Opp. to BSNL, Near Chennoth Glass, Palarivattom,
Ernakulam - 682 025. Phones: 0484-3205797, 2535636
- TC 27/2162, Chirakulam Road, Statue,
Thiruvananthapuram - 695 001. Phone: 0471-2570445
- 3638/A, IVth Cross, Opp. to Malleswaram Railway Station,
Gayathri Nagar, Back gate of Subramaniya Nagar,
Bengalooru - 560 021. Phone: 080-23324950

Printed at T. Krishna Press, Chennai - 600 102 and Published by V.V.K.Subburaj for First Edition [An imprint of Sura Books (Pvt) Ltd.] 1620, 'J' Block, 16th Main Road, Anna Nagar, Chennai - 600 040. Phones: 26162173, 26161099. Fax: (91) 44-26162173.
e-mail: enquiry@surabooks.com; website: www.surabooks.com

02 10 1000

PREFACE

The women whose life stories fill these pages were exceptional in more ways than one.

Exceptional in their resolve and undaunting will. Exceptional in their spirit of service to mankind.

The mettle they were made of had a unique blend of the tough and the tender.

Why do so few of us make it to the 'top'? Remember, ascents involve many obstacles and only those who have the grit to surmount hurdles are able to elevate themselves in spirit and stature.

Why write on women personalities?

The women chosen here are representatives of the age in which they lived and worked. Success for women was never easy in a male-dominated world, more so in early times. Men faced fewer challenges, be it at home or at work.

Florence Nightingale silently rebels against the near useless and wasted life of a young girl belonging to a wealthy family. Labouring against parental opposition, she chooses the much neglected and forbidden area of hospitals to work in.

Maria Montessori braved ridicule to be the only girl student in a boy's medical school. We read about the glaring social inequalities that confronted her repeatedly. Yet she became the first woman to get a medical degree in the whole of Italy.

In a sense these women were pathbreakers.

Mother Teresa, of course, makes her choice of renunciation early in life. Success was for her sacrifice, service to the poor and a charitable disposition. No marriage, but an intense dedication to work. By nursing the wounds on the bodies of the sick and old human beings, she directly manages to heal her own soul!

We all make the most of whatever nature gives us. But in Helen Keller's case, nature had not been too generous. Yet she fought the odds in the most hopeless of situations. Help to her came in the form of another notable woman – Anne Sullivan.

They take tough decisions. In 1873, Annie Besant had to either conform and attend the Communion or had to leave home. She chose the latter. That is the price she paid for her freedom and opted for an uncertain future.

Marie Curie's sense of self-worth must have been tremendous as her husband Pierre was much ahead of his times and he never contemplated his wife giving up her work or research. How she juggled between the pressures of home and work is another story of courage. She was encouraged and helped tremendously by all the three men in her life - her father, her husband and her father-in-law. As a couple, both aroused appreciation all over the world!

Life stories usually become a chronology of events and the reasons behind certain actions or decisions, with time, get neglected or totally obliterated. Take the case of Indira Gandhi. Her possessiveness as a child coupled with her desire to protect her parents gets large enough with time and age to accommodate an entire nation. With parents no more on the scene she feels that same passionate urge to defend her country.

Another factor common among these women is that they are relatively free of any prejudice. Far from it, they worked in lands away from their place of birth. The greatness of their work cuts across geographic boundaries, be it Mother Teresa, Madame Curie or Annie Besant.

Their childhood events reveal the impact on them in later years. The straggles, the economic hardships, the restrictions, the tremendous self-control and their sensitivities – all of which leaves a trail on them, making them individualistic in dealing with life's problems. Of course, in each of them we get a glimpse of the brief, but impressionable, role of the mother, father and siblings also.

Every generation is judged by their succeeding generations. Evaluation is also comparative but, if after repeated re-evaluations, you emerge on "top", then you are invaluable. These women surface again and again. Need I say more?

Their lives being exemplary, I hope readers will enrich themselves by the wisdom filtered out of them. May the essence of their experiences alter perceptions for good and those who are divorced from inspiration may yet find reconciliation, once again, in these stories.

All beings have a right to utilize their full potential. Even women.

It was a pleasure writing about them.

VINITA

CONTENTS

FAMOUS *Women* PERSONALITIES

MOTHER TERESA

A face deeply lined, twinkling eyes and hands folded in prayer with utmost humility. Fingers that got twisted and feet that became rugged with the strenuous and tough life she led. Draped in an ordinary white cotton sari with a blue border. That is the familiar image of the 'sister of the slums' – whom everyone knows as Mother Teresa.

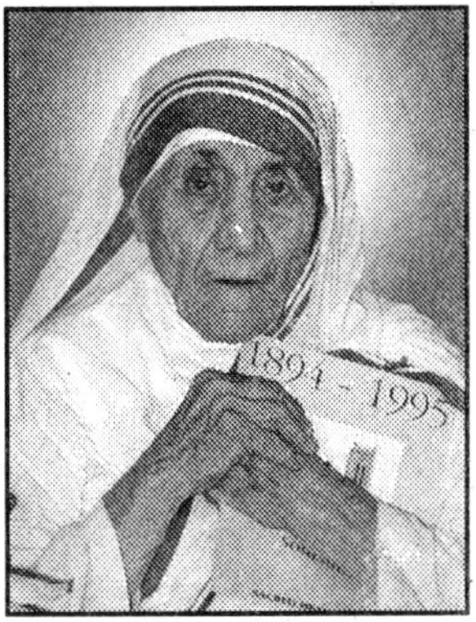

Born on August 26th 1910 in Skopje into an Albanian family, Mother Teresa was the youngest child of Nicholas Bojaxhiu and Dranafile Bernai. She was christened Agnes Gonxha Bojaxhiu when she was just a day old. In Albanian, Gonxha means 'flower bud.' As a child she was pink and plump. She had a neat and tidy appearance and was helpful always even then.

Her elder sister Age was born in 1904 and Lazar, her elder brother in 1907. They lived in a large house with a large garden full of fruit trees. Her father was a building contractor while her mother was from Venice. Hers was a closely knit happy family.

Mother Teresa was very close to her mother. Her spiritual life was greatly influenced by her mother's strong sense of values and her commitment to faith. The children called their mother 'Nana Loke' meaning, the mother of my soul. Her father too was of a charitable disposition.

Her mother was against the wasting of resources. There is a story about their childhood, when the three siblings sat around their mother chatting playfully. Their mother quietly listened for a long time then abruptly got up and switched off the lights saying electricity should not be wasted on foolish talk.

Her elder brother Lazar also recounts how he would get up at odd hours in the night to steal jam. Though Gonxha would tell him not to do so, she would never go and complain to their mother.

Her mother was strict but was also very kind. She would visit the poor and the needy with food and money. Agnes, as a little girl would love to go with her mother. They were taught to pray regularly and love and care those in need.

Sadly and quite suddenly their father died. Her mother, after being struck with grief was at first unable to come to grips with the tragedy. She remained in a kind of stupor, while Age, her eldest daughter took the responsibility of the family. After she recovered, she started a small business of her own to earn enough to bring up her three children. They had nothing but a house of their own.

Her mother worked hard, sewing wedding dresses and making embroidered stuff. In spite of such hardships, their mother found time to spend with her children and teach them good things.

Both Agnes and her elder sister Age, were in the choir and participated in many activities of the church. Agnes did very well in school and she was fond of reading and writing too. In fact her brother thought she would make a career out of writing.

But destiny had other plans. She was only twelve years old when she first felt the desire to become a nun. As she was still a child her mother did not agree but many hours did they spend together in the church, praying and in other such activities.

From Father Jambrenkovic she learned about the lives of saints and missionaries and about the experiences they had with the people and children of India. She learnt about the Loreto order of nuns who were working in Bengal, educating children. All this had a great impact on Agnes.

By the time Agnes turned eighteen, she had made up her mind that she wanted to become a missionary in India. For this, she had to become a nun and join the Irish order of the sisters of Loreto. This time, her mother understood her daughter's deep inner desire to serve the poor and advised her to have faith in God and He would lead her on. As nuns in those days could not visit home she knew she would never see her daughter again.

Agnes turned to father Jambren Kovic to remove her doubts about this inner Call of God. He explained to her that such Calls of God came with a sense of inner joy. Still in her teens, Agnes' only aim in life was to become a humble Loreto nun.

In September of 1928, Agnes with her mother and sister left Skopje for Zagreb by train. After the interview in Paris, Agnes along with another girl were send to Dublin in Ireland where they had to learn English and were trained as nuns. Both the girls quietly and obediently underwent the training for several weeks. Then in December 28 , the two girls started for the long journey to India by ship.

On the twenty third of May 1929 Agnes changed her name to Teresa after the name of a French Carmalite nun and on May 24th 1931, she took her first temporary vows of poverty, charity and obedience.

When she arrived in India in January 1929 she was sent to the novitiate at the hill resort of Darjeeling where the surrounding natural scenery was proof of God's power and beauty. Her life as a novice began here, in the Himalayas, below the snow covered Mount Kanchenjunga.

Here during her two year stay she began to learn Bengali and picked up some Hindi too. She soon began to be called the "Bengali Teresa" because she had mastered this language so well. For two hours each day they also taught poor children and she also liked helping at the hospital. There she saw the suffering of the poor, the kind she had never even imagined.

After Sister Teresa's time was up, she had to leave the fresh air of the mountain side to go and live in the Loreto Sisters' compound at Entally. At St. Mary's in the same compound she taught history and geography and was wonderful as a teacher.

After Sister Teresa took her final lifetime vows in 1937, she was a professed nun at last and was made principal of St. Mary's School.

People recall, that even then she was a very dedicated and charitable worker. She was witty with a fine sense of humour. Sometimes while enjoying jokes she would bend double with laughter.

The political events and the Second World War changed the pace of the lives of the inmates of the Convent. There were raids on Calcutta. In 1942, the Loreto Complex at Entally was converted into a temporary military hospital, and St. Mary's School was shifted to a building on Convent Road.

Then in 1942-43 the Great Famine broke out. Burmese rice was cut off because of the Japanese invasion. Prices rose and many died on the streets. In 1946, communal tension between Hindus and Muslims became the reason for a nightmare of violence that killed more than four thousand people within five days.

During the riots once, Sister Teresa went out to find food for her students. She was horrified at the bloodshed she saw. Soldiers instantly stopped her but Sister Teresa was only concerned about the needs of her pupils and not about her own safety. The soldiers then helped her to find the rice for her three hundred students and even delivered it inside the school.

The misery of the refugees in Calcutta and the ghastly state of the Motijhil slum affected her deeply.

Then came God's call. The message she said was very clear to her : to leave the convent and help the poor while living among them. It was an order. 'A call within a call.' This was

September 1946 on her way by train to Darjeeling where once every year the Sisters would go up in the hills to pray in quietness. She spoke to a priest about this and though he was quite stunned he said he would speak to the Archbishop.

On the 8th of August 1948, Father Van Exem was permitted by the Archbishop to break the news to Mother Teresa that she could leave the Order and go and live in the slums. She wrote to her mother in Skopje to inform her that she had taken permission from the Vatican and she was leaving with her religious vows intact.

On 17th August 1948 Mother Teresa wore her new dress, the white sari with the blue border which Father Van Exem had blessed together with a small cross and rosary. Though she was given an emotional farewell by children singing Bengali songs no one saw her leave when she slipped out of the Convent in Entally.

She then lived with the Medical Mission Sisters in Patna for a few months to learn about nursing and outdoor dispensary work. She was taught to give injections, medicines and even to help in child birth. After her short stay in Patna was over, she returned to Calcutta, where she found a temporary shelter with the Little Sisters of the poor.

The Medical Missionaries of Patna asked her to feed her Sisters well and not keep them on a diet of rice and salt as Mother Teresa was determined to do. The nuns then would suffer and not be strong to serve the sick and poor. Mother Teresa did follow their advice and made sure later that the young girls joining her had a proper breakfast of chapattis before they left for work in the mornings. But the sisters accepted no money or refreshments, not even a cup of tea in gratitude. According to them gratitude could not be material when the service was for God.

Mother Teresa felt poverty was her strength and her freedom. She had stepped out of Cacutta's Loreto with a five rupee note, three saris and a huge amount of faith.

When she stepped in Motijhil, the bustee from where she began, she felt the children needed a school. She did not have a building and tables and chairs. So she just picked up a stick from the ground and drew figures and alphabets on a small patch of land. Few children gathered around at once and the following days more and more came. Someone donated a couple of chairs and a blackboard. The school had started! She would teach personal hygiene and cleanliness. Regular students were awarded soap cakes as prizes. They got milk at mid day.

Her state was pathetic those days as she tried to uplift the state of the poor and show to them the glory of God's love. Without helpers, how could her solitary efforts help to give relief to so many suffering humans?

Her prayers were answered and got her a house, helpers and her first task was to build and train her team. Michael Gomes, who lived with his family in 14, Creek Lane, offered her the use of the second floor of his house. This house became a haven of peace and love for her. In March 1949, at the door stood a frail figure in front of her, saying she wanted to join Mother. She was prepared for the tough life ahead. She was Sister Agnes, the first candidate to join Mother and to trust the inspiration that was behind such saintly work. Mother never forgot this fact and the two shared a special bond of friendship. After a few weeks, another candidate joined and then yet another one joined to work with her. Mother was overjoyed as the number of helpers kept increasing.

Mother was like a saint in their midst showing them the purpose of the institute. The sisters always listened attentively and with full admiration to Mother Teresa. The sisters prayed, studied, cooked, washed clothes, scrubbed floors and prepared bandages. The list of candidates wanting to join Mother, was growing and so was the number of member sisters.

Mother Teresa then took Indian citizenship. She wrote out very carefully the aims of her little group and the Rule that they followed. The Archbishop was impressed and the constitution was accepted on October 7, 1950 and the Missionaries of Charity were recognised by the Catholic Church and also approved by the Pope.

Mother states that a missionary of charity must be a missionary of love. She must be full of charity in her own soul and spread the same charity to the souls of others, Christians and non Christians.

More and more applications were coming in and the house, second floor at 14, Creek Lane was getting full. She felt it was a signal from God to prepare to spread out the efforts of the sisters throughout the world.

A generous Muslim, a friend of Father Van Exem provided Mother Teresa with her first proper Motherhouse of her Order. It is a place of great calm and peace, where the Sisters can rest before and after their work.

Soon help started coming from the Archbishop Calcutta, the Chief Minister of West Bengal and later from the Prime Minister of India, many friends not only from India but from groups of ladies from America and Britain. Some sent supplies of foodstuffs and medicines while her work was praised in the press.

Mother Teresa never complained of any hardship and God's praise was always on her lips. She disliked wastage of things. Often during her early days she would go hungry so that someone else could get a meal. At times she would donate her tram fare and walk back home. She would get the unwanted food collected for the poor during her plane trips. Feasts to be given in her honour were cancelled and she would instead take the money that was to be spent, for the poor. There were no fans for the chapels or for the common room that was used by the Sisters of Charity.

Mother Teresa offered to take care of the homeless destitute, sick, starving, those dying on the streets. Her first major work was the Kalighat Home for the Dying. The home, or hospital was called 'Nirmal Hriday.' It has two wards that can take in as many as sixty men and sixty women. Thousands died in the home, decently, peacefully, and prayerfully. The Sisters with their helpers, washed and fed them, consoled them, cheered their spirits and prepared their souls so that each one of them could die in peace.

For the care of orphans, of abandoned children and crippled children Shishu Bhavan, the Children's Home in Calcutta was started.

Since then it has been for many years the centre of varied activities ranging from being a home to abandoned children and cripples to being a home for unwedded mothers to stay while expecting their child. There are also stores of food that are given free to the poor.

There is an interesting story about a woman who came to Mother Teresa to pray for her husband so that he may stop drinking. He was having one whisky bottle per day costing ninety rupees.

Mother said if he can spend so much on a whisky bottle I will spend five hundred per month to start a children's home.

She was asked what the reasoning was by Father Le Joly, she said – "You men go by logic. We women follow our intuition and we are more often right than you."

Yes, he agreed; because insight is based on love and so is correct as compared to dry logic.

This is how the house for Shishu Bhavan was rented.

Mother Teresa started working for the welfare of leprosy patients. She started a Leprosy Collection Day. Collection tins were taken around Calcutta for Mother Teresa's Leprosy fund with the slogan 'Touch the Leper with your kindness.' Money poured in from all sources.

Shanti Nagar, the Town of Peace was founded as a colony and rehabilitation centre for lepers in the district of Burdwan.

Mother, with her Sisters brought hope to the people in God's goodness.

The Children's Home in Delhi was inaugurated by the Prime Minister, Mr. Nehru and the Swiss Ambassador Mr. Cuttat. Mr. Nehru surprised them by telling that he already knew about the work they were doing and that was the reason why he came for the inauguration.

In December 1979, Mother Teresa went to Norway to receive the highest award, the Nobel Peace Prize. She felt happy as she thought the world was recognizing the poor whom she served. The entire money of the award was to be used to feed the starving and build homes for the homeless and for the lepers.

In 1964 when the Pope visited India, he gifted his beautiful white Rolls Royce to her before he left. Mother Teresa auctioned it to get more money for the poor.

In 1973, she was given a huge, building which she named 'Prem Daan' or 'Gift of Love'. Here too the sick and demented are cared for. Prem Daan is used as a home for those who have a better chance to recover and survive; they are kept there for a longer period of time if the need be, till they are well enough to be on their own feet. Other types of needy persons are also looked after here. Kalighat remains a home for the dying destitute who have little chances of surviving.

In 1963, the Brother's Branch was started because for certain kinds of work, men were more suited as they could even better handle the grown up boys at Shishu Bhavan which the Sisters would have difficulty in dealing with as also in the work with the leprosy patients. In 1963 the first brothers came from all over the world, giving up everything, to join Mother Teresa in her work for the poor and the needy. By the year 1976, there were one hundred and seventy five Brothers working for the welfare of juvenile delinquents, drug addicts, lepers and the mental patients. They do not look like priests but they wear simple clothes and go about their way of serving in a most gentle and kind manner.

Mother Teresa's work by this time was noticed all over the country. Branches of her schools, hospitals and clinics were springing up rapidly. She thought it was time to look beyond the continent and to work for the poor of the entire world.

In 1965, the Pope Paul VI allowed the Missionaries of Charity to work outside India for the first time. Mother opened a mission in Ceylon, in Venezuela and she also visited Rome.

In March 1991, Mother opened a house in Albania. Gradually she opened eight houses to meet the spiritual needs of the people there and to bring back religious knowledge and it's practice.

Mother was by birth an Albanian but she felt sad that for many years she was not allowed to visit Albania because the country was ruled by a strict dictator, Enver Hodja. Though he was born in a Muslim family, he was a fanatic and did not believe in God, he stopped all religious practices and killed priests or jailed them. He closed all mosques and churches and declared Albania an atheistic state. It was only after his death that people rejoiced and prayed without the fear of being put in jail.

Then Mother visited her homeland. She even met the widow of the departed leader and went to pray at his tomb. She was also handed over the key to the Catholic Cathedral which she gave to the priest.

Mother once said that God had given her strong health and a good constitution. She ate very little and still she would be up from four in the morning and working the whole day. But a time did come when her health was being over taxed. She suffered a heart attack in 1983. She also developed cataract in both the eyes. In 1989 she got a second attack and a pace maker was fitted. Still she went back to her work. But in January 1997, she did not agree to serve another term when the electors came as she was not feeling well.

Mother Teresa's last day was 5th of September in 1997. She had not been feeling well again and did not want to go to a Nursing Home either. She could see that her life on earth was coming to an end so she expressed her wish to die in the house. Around nine at night she said that she was unable to breathe. By the time the doctor came she had passed away.

Sister Nirmala Joshi had become her successor and Mother Teresa had blessed her in office and had even introduced her to the Sisters.

October 19th of the year 2003 was the date of beatification of Mother Teresa. This date coincides with three important events :

1. 25th anniversary of the election of Pope John Paul II
2. World Mission Sunday
3. Conclusion of the year of the Rosary.

The first thing that would strike just about anyone was Mother Teresa's littleness and her humble presence. But her activities were amazingly big! She would prefer to work than to spend time in long sessions of meetings which resulted in nothing. After she attended one such meeting, she said she felt "like a fish out of water".

She took quick decisions, worked fast and all her activities were marked with a kind of dynamism. She was sensitive to the needs of the suffering and instantly worked out the solution.

When she saw a man dying on the streets, she opened a home for the dying. The sight of abandoned children made her start Shishu Bhavan. When people ignored the problem of the colony of lepers, she worked for leprosy in a big way. In the face of any calamity, be it a famine or an earthquake she was always there to distribute supplies. She trained the slum children, she asked people to use the coconut shells lying waste on the roads to make ropes.

Once, when questioned about the problem of raising money, she replied, "I never think of it. It always comes. The Lord sends it. We do His work; He provides the means. If he does not give us the means that shows that He does not want the work. So why worry?"

Her trust in God was complete. After years of such belief in unseen things she had lived it out for others to see and feel till it became a reality, a fact of life.

It was not that she always met with success in her attempts. The Missionaries of Charity also had to face quite a few failures. Mother thanked God for them also. In Simla the sisters opened a house there in the hill station. Their clothing was not adapted for the cold weather and opportunity for doing spiritual work were far less. Losing heart, they soon left the place.

After being invited to Colombo, The Missionaries of Charity were asked to leave and go back to India.

At Ranchi the people were determined not to allow her to occupy the land she had acquired for her foundation. When she reached there she was met with cries of, "Go back, Mother Teresa." She tried talking to them, but it was of no help and they had to turn back.

The local people's interests and fears have to be also kept in mind while choosing a location as she later realised. A peaceful solution was found by shifting a children's home to the new property and then shifting out the home for the dying destitute to the old home of children.

At Cuttack, Mother suffered a personal defeat when she tried to settle a quarrel between the laity, some priests and the hierarchy.

There was opposition also during the opening of Nirmal Hriday. The Home was on the sacred temple ground. Kalighat temple, served by nearly four hundred priests, is immensely popular. A group of people were of the opinion that Mother was coming to a holy place of the Hindus to convert people to Christianity.

But her loving heart gladly withstood such obstacles without bitterness or any jealousy.

When Mother went to the Vatican with Sister Nirmala, for a private meeting with Pope John Paul, he blessed her and gave advice with paternal affection. Mother Teresa introduced the new Superior General to him. She said, "And I, now, I am a nobody."

The Pope replied, "You are the Foundress."

Her humility was present up to the very end. No one can ever take away the honourable title of the Foundress of the Missionaries of Charity as the Pope had said. That is her very own just as her mission for love was her own when she first started life outside the convent gates.

⌘ ❖ ⌘

FLORENCE NIGHTINGALE

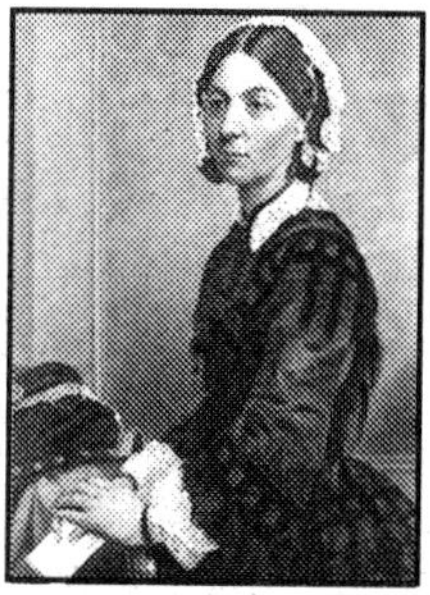

The nursing profession today owes a lot to the invaluable contribution of Florence Nightingale. She was a pioneer in the nursing field. Before she started her work, nurses were largely untrained. They considered their job a lowly chore. They were not caring and gentle like the nurses of today but were careless and dirty. People looked down upon nurses and women from good families did not enter this profession.

Hospitals were so dirty that people were scared to go there. The bed linen and mattresses were hardly changed from one patient to the next. The floors were not cleaned and scrubbed while the walls stank with dampness. Patients with infectious diseases were not kept in a separate ward. Doctors too practised no hygiene before surgery.

Florence Nightingale, with her efforts, raised the standards of not just the nursing but the medical profession as well.

Florence Nightingale was born in Florence, Italy on May 12th 1820. She was a remarkable woman, tough as well as bright, a brilliant organizer and one of the most influential women in the 19th Century England.

Nightingale was raised mostly in Derbyshire, England and received a thorough classical education from her father.

By the time she was eighteen years old, she was pretty and intelligent both. She enjoyed her lessons in Greek, French, History and Philosophy that her father, Mr. Nightingale wanted her to undergo. In fact she excelled in them while her sister Parenthope, who was a year older than her was most unlike the studious Florence.

When Florence Nightingale was eighteen years old, their family explored Europe. It was a very enjoyable and exciting trip. Such journeys by horse driven coaches were strenuous but they were full of adventure. On the south coast of France, in Nice and in Genoa, Florence enjoyed the music and the balls which they attended. Next they visited Florence, the city where Florence Nightingale was born. The palaces and churches fascinated her considerably, while the paintings and statues she saw, were equally beautiful.

Florence would carefully keep her diaries. She would record in great detail whatever she saw and all that was of interest to her. Even the date and time of events were accurately observed.

Florence was very good looking, graceful, witty and full of life. The brother of her best friend, Marianne, wanted to marry her. His name was Henry Nicholson. Florence's mother, Fanny wanted her lovely daughter to marry well and hoped the day would soon arrive.

In those days, young ladies were bred to be gentle and demure. They spent their time reading books, listening to music or doing embroidery work.

Florence was very fond of music. She loved concerts, operas, balls and dancing. Sometimes she would dance till the early hours of the morning enjoying the music and gaiety.

Rich women mostly spent their lives dressing fashionably visiting operas where young men noticed them. But Florence saw the uselessness of leading life in such a manner.

Born into an aristocratic family, Florence Nightingale felt that her talents would be wasted if she just played the role of a typical Victorian lady, that of wife and mother. In spite of her well to do life style Florence was suffering within. Most men did not approve of ambitious and outspoken women. Being educated and concerned about social issues she knew the problems that would come in her future life. What was to be her life in such narrowed circumstances? Questioning her own self repeatedly, and thinking about solutions where none existed, she would get extremely depressed. With the passage of time, she started keeping ill health and her family thought it was a good idea to send her to stay with her Aunt Mai in London. They probably felt Florence was bored and a change in socialising would be good to cure her of her gloom.

Florence was still tired of the same routine. She had become fluent in many languages and would continue with her studies of Greek and mathematics in her bedroom upstairs for long hours. Aunt Mai understood Florence's need to pursue something challenging, so agreed to let her have her way. She wanted Florence to be happy. When Fanny heard about her daughter's interest in mathematics, she was very annoyed. What had mathematics to do with looking after the household, a thing which she hoped Florence would do once she was married? This time Florence was adamant. Yet she felt as though her life was frittering away without any aim.

Once during summer she visited the country home and saw the great difference in the lives of the rich and the poor. She saw starvation of young girls who worked all day and also at night by the light of mere candles. She saw how on the other hand the wealthy dined heartily absolutely unaware of the misery of the poor.

She was a sensitive, thinking and concerned human being. The sight of suffering changed her. She was already suffocating under the weight of the dance and dine routine and would often sink in gloom. She wanted to help the needy and her mind too was absorbed with that idea. But in those times it was certainly not considered proper to do so.

She set her sights on nursing as an outlet for her talents, at the age of twenty-four. She wanted to work with the sick in hospitals. She was one of the first women to break out of the Victorian traditional mould. Her family was horrified and rejected the idea totally because respectable women did not become nurses.

However, an American Philanthropist, Dr. Samuel Howe encouraged her and advised her to pursue her ambitions. But Florence knew that she would have to undertake training and learn nursing before serving the sick.

With a sense of determination, she secretly began to study about hospital management and how to improve the conditions of hospitals. She would request some of her friends to send her information about German and French hospitals too. She would be busy working and writing at her desk till odd hours in the morning. Her family remained unaware of her determination to pursue this profession as Florence spent a normal dull day, downstairs with her family. She kept putting off all talks of her marriage. Her friends and family were quite keen that she marry Henry Nicholson.

When Florence was twenty-six she received information about an institution of Deaconesses – ladies, who were more like nuns, in Germany where they nursed the sick.

Florence saw hope and felt her parents and family would agree to this work.

But she could not still gather courage to mention it to her parents. Meanwhile after much effort she refused all pressures for marriage because she wanted nothing to prevent her from a life of service. Her mother was of course extremely angry. There was another man who was quite intelligent and whom Florence adored. He was Richard Monckton Milnes whom she met in the year 1842. Even though she was heartbroken, she refused marriage to him because she realised she would never be content looking after the children and her household. She had a very deep desire to be of service to society. She plunged into despair once more and so her family thought it best that she go for a holiday to recover.

Florence decided to take an educational tour of Egypt with her friends. Though she read and took down notes and took an interest in all she saw, her mind was filled with a sense of sadness. This vexed state actually renewed her determination and towards the end of July she reached Kaiserswerth in Germany. There at a local hospital she spent a fortnight with the Christian women nursing the sick.

She wrote about those religious women and the work they were doing, so that other women too would be persuaded to give up an idle life of affluent homes and join similar activities.

When she reached home, her mother was furious and told her that she had disgraced the family. Florence may have failed in this endeavour, but she did in the end decide to go into nursing, no matter what her family thought. She knew by now that she would get no sympathy from her family. Meanwhile, Parthe grew more and more sick so her parents felt that Florence should devote more time to her sister and not be selfish about her freedom. Florence patiently nursed her sister for six months and then she went to stay with Sydney Herbert and his wife who understood her desire to become a nurse. She also met the first woman to become a doctor, Dr. Elizabeth and that gave her fresh hope as she now thought it was possible for women to achieve their ambitions.

Florence went for a three month stay at Kaiserswerth though her family did not let anyone know about it. There she lived a tough life, eating a simple and small meal and praying at short intervals. Yet she was filled with a new kind of joy. After her stay she came back with her mother and sister to find her father at home ill with a painful eye. Florence not only had to look after him but also had to take him for treatment. During the journey he understood his daughter's feeling and was now like a friend to her unlike her sister and mother.

In the year 1853 when Florence Nightingale was thirty-three years old she took up the job of Superintendent at the Institution for the care of sick Gentlewomen in London. This news made her mother and sister weep and get angry but Florence was adamant. Her father then granted her an allowance to take up her own rooms in London and be independent.

With full enthusiasm Florence started to reorganize the hospital. Soiled and stinking bed linen were removed, brooms and dusters were bought, she installed hardworking house keepers and in a short span of time she became a specialist in her field. She was loved by both patients and women because of her sympathetic nature.

Florence wanted efficient workers. She was taking revolutionary decisions so many even opposed her. But there was a kind of a genius in her and her sharp mind and keen sense of observation was admired by many. Initially the committee was aghast by her list of requirements but they were also very impressed by her ideas of improvement and her performance in the administration of the hospital.

Florence, meanwhile distanced herself from her family and took her own decisions. She concentrated on her job and started planning how to recruit daughters of farmers to join nursing. She wanted to train them like the ladies she had observed at Kaiserworth.

Meanwhile the British Army in the Crimea was fighting with France to support their Turkish allies in a war with Russia. Though the British troops were gallant they had to battle with the epidemic cholera and over one thousand died of that disease.

The soldiers battling in the Crimea were tired, thirsty and suffering from disease. The number of casualties were appalling. The wounded had to wait for many days lying on the coast, waiting for some ship to transport them to the hospital on the South Coast of the Black Sea. The journey was full of hardships and many died because of infection of the wounds.

There were no bandages, supplies or medicines to help the wounded. The surgeons operated in moonlight as there were no lamps or candles. The open ground was covered with dirt and there were no anaesthetics. These sick and wounded soldiers were sent to Scutari. But the hospital there was already overflowing with the cholera infected and had to make room for 1500 more battle wounded soldiers. So the hospital could provide no food since there was no kitchen.

The Barrack hospital was a bare building with men lying on the floor with no beds, no operating tables, nor any food supply for the sick. The question before Great Britain was, that who was to nurse the wounded and the suffering as the French had the Sisters of Charity to help in the war field.

An old friend of Florence, Sydney Herbert sent a letter to her asking her to go to Scutari urgently. He was then Secretary of War and asked Florence to arrange for a group of nurses to take with her to Scutari as soon as it was possible.

Florence accepted the task and with forty nurses she set out as Superintendent of the Female Nursing Establishment of the English General Hospitals in Turkey.

This time her family fully supported her as they realized that perhaps, Florence was made to do this great and noble work.

Florence reached the Barrack Hospital in Scutari on November 5, 1854. Florence had prepared herself for the worst, but what met her eyes stunned her. There was misery, dirt and rubbish every where. She and her nurses had to start work but very carefully. Signed permission slips had to be taken from doctors and any nurse who did not follow this rule was sent back home. Florence forced herself to follow the rules as she knew she would not be able to help the soldiers without winning the trust of the doctors who simply ignored her. So Florence took upon her to look after the food and the kitchen. But things changed on November 9, when hundreds of battle wounded and diseased came to Scutari. Now the doctors could not ignore Florence and her nurses as they needed their help and assistance.

Florence attended to each soldier, dressed their wounds, saw that they bathed and wore clean clothes and ate a good meal. Remember when she took over, the hospital was a rats and flea infested area, with no furniture and no lamps either. Soldiers were regarded as brutes by their officers.

Florence fought against all odds to improve the conditions and to provide help from private donations and charities in Britain to get supplies of essential goods.

The soldiers loved her saintly and kindly presence. She became famous as "The Lady with the Lamp" because she made her rounds at night holding a Turkish lamp. A soldier wrote home about how comforting her presence was, so much so that they kissed her shadow as she passed them.

Some felt soldiers had to be used to a tough life and Florence was actually spoiling them by such gentle treatment.

When the situation at Scutari was well under control she would often ride and go, even in rough weather, to visit the battle areas and inspect the medical stations that were there.

The British were defeated at the Battle of Balaclava. The camp that was there nearby was filthy and stinking. Dead bodies and amputated limbs of the wounded soldiers floated in the sea. Cholera spread fast within the army. The Battle of Inkermann followed. The British were victorious but many soldiers were blinded, wounded and crippled. Their lives depended on good care and clean conditions in the hospital. It was like a flood of the diseased which Florence tried hard to jam in every space. They were suffering from dysentery and gangrene. She had to struggle against such odds. In November, a storm broke out and swept away the tents of the army to make matters worse.

In January 1855 the state of the wounded became a kind of calamity and patients multiplied at an alarming rate. Four doctors and three nurses also died within a span of two weeks. The water supply too was infected. Besides there was hardly any protection from the freezing cold weather.

Florence worked relentlessly but these long working hours made her very ill and weak. She became very thin and pale but as her Aunt Mai observed that she had attained a wonderful calm. Florence's mother also wrote to her telling her how proud she felt of the work she was doing.

In England, Florence had become the heroine of the Crimean war and a lot of money was raised and received in her name through various means; so a Nightingale Fund was set up. The money was used to establish a training institute for nurses. Even the troop's donated one day's pay to the fund. The market was full of Nightingale pottery, like mugs and plates, poems were written and even a life boat was named after her.

Peace was declared on April 29th 1856. Florence then returned to England. By now she had become a celebrity and was constantly flooded with letters admiring and congratulating her. But she was quite unmoved and attended no public functions.

Her work was hardly over. In fact this was just the first step of the forty years ahead of active work which she put in. Florence wanted to reform the hospitals, their administration and even the health and living conditions of the entire country of India. She wanted to start with the British Army. She proved that the death rate of soldiers was more during peace time as compared to the average population. The army recruited healthy young men who were not killed by war but by gross neglect of their health, food and living conditions. The people supported her moves for reform totally. Change did not come completely but she did manage to rebuild some barracks and reduce the death rate by fifty percent.

Just two months after her return from the Crimea, Florence went to Balmoral in Scotland where she met the Queen and Prince Albert. She had gone there because the Queen had expressed a desire to listen to her story from her own lips. After hearing all she put before them, the Queen wrote to her Commander in Chief to let Florence work at the war office. So Florence with the help of Sydney Herbert, spent another six months working hard on her hospital visits and writing her research work. She was more accurate, more experienced, brighter and could easily persuade people about her plans.

She prepared a one thousand page report, Notes on Matters affecting Health, Efficiency and Hospital Administration of the British Army.

Soon, all over the world, Florence became an expert on the building of hospitals. More windows and better ventilation resulted and the drainage system was improved. Laundry rooms and clean kitchens also became a part of her style of hospitals.

When we visit hospitals today and see them sparkling and cheerful, we know all this is a result of the efforts put in by the courageous and intelligent lady – Florence Nightingale.

In 1859 she published 'Notes on Nursing: what it is and what it is not.' It was a revolutionary work where, besides hygiene and basic health, she wrote about the need for a sensitive approach to the suffering of the sick person. Today this is accepted as a slogan for all medical institutions.

Her 'Nightingale Training School' was a success. There was a demand worldwide for Nightingale nurses. They were disciplined, given neat uniforms and had a room for themselves. Gradually nursing got transformed into a respectable profession.

In 1860 Florence lost her dear friend Sydney Herbert, who had given her the opportunity to serve the war office. They had worked together for the cause of Army Reform.

But by now Florence was not keeping good health herself. Working day and night she had become frail and suffered a collapse. The American Civil War had broken out and her help was needed. She could not walk so she conducted her work, to give advice and instruction, lying on a sofa. For many years she remained one of the most persons since politicians and hospital administrators consulted her regularly and she proved to be a brilliant administrator with her innovative ideas.

Then Florence turned her attention towards improving the health of the country – India. She observed that soldiers in India died not by the heat but by poor drainage and unclean water. She prepared a two thousand page report and she wrote to every medical officer in India. But she had wanted to do more for the poor and ordinary in India and felt reforms were taking too long.

In 1880 Florence lost her mother Fanny and her sister Partha died in 1890. In their final years Florence had nursed them very patiently. In old age too, Florence was calm, firm and kind. She was loved by the young nurses whom she enjoyed interviewing. Then her eyes began to fail till she could see nothing at all.

In November 1907, King Edward VII awarded Florence Nightingale the Order of Merit. The order was given to a woman for the first time. But Florence was very weak by then and the Order was delivered to her house in London, she fell asleep after murmuring "Too kind, too kind."

At her age of ninety on August 13th 1910 when Florence went to sleep it was forever. She passed away in her sleep.

She liked simplicity so, in keeping with her wishes Florence was given a quiet burial near the family's home at Embley. Her coffin was carried by six sergeants of the British Army. Of course entire bus-loads of nurses reached her funeral in 1910, to pay their tributes to the lovable soul. After all it was the perseverance of this one lady called Florence Nightingale who had given such a respectable standard to their profession.

Just three months before Florence died, the Jubilee of the Nightingale Training School for Nurses was held at New York's Carnegie Hall. Florence's achievements were acknowledged there because by that time within United States alone, there existed more than 1000 training schools.

Florence Nightingale changed and shaped the role of women of her time. She derived great joy from the letters she received from around the globe. She made people change their attitudes towards soldiers. She sensitized people towards childbirth, the poor and the sick and suffering. Hospital buildings underwent major reforms. She enabled wide-ranging workhouse reforms by pressing for an Act of Parliament.

Queen Victoria had a deep admiration for Nightingale's achievements in the Crimean War and she supported her campaign for reform of the army health service.

Florence Nightingale was one of God's most gifted beings. She was a perfectionist yet she had a very gentle voice and manner. Her clarity of mind and inner strength were extraordinary. Every time we see a hospital, to our mind comes the picture of 'The Lady with the Lamp' who was the founder of it all – nursing, preventive medicine, cleanliness and good food – all proved with a long and thorough research!

⌘ ❖ ⌘

ANNIE BESANT

Annie Besant is often described in one word as a theosophist. Some stress upon her role as an educator when a great many others, value her intense devotion to India and to the people of India.

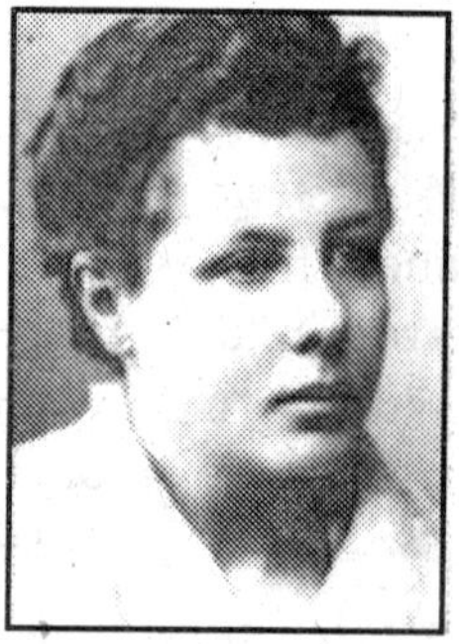

All these descriptions about her are very much correct, but they miss out a very important factor. Her whole life was actually a story of courage and a search for Truth. Her loyalty to Truth was so great that she said she would follow it no matter where it led her, and even after her death she wanted the line, "She tried to follow Truth", as her epitaph on her tomb.

Born on October 1, 1847 as Annie Wood in Claphem, London, her parents were William Wood and Emily Morris. Her mother was of pure Irish descent, while her father was half Irish.

She loved the Irish language, it was like music to her ears. The nature of the Irish too, according to her was specially unique in its warmth and friendliness. Even the poorest worn out woman on the road would reply in a bright and friendly manner when asked anything. Blessings poured from every tongue, which was a good way of being guided in life. In no other nation had she seen such natural qualities present even in the most ordinary of natives. The reason for this, she felt, was probably because Ireland was a land that had been inhabited by men of wisdom and she saw it as an Island of Saints.

Annie Besant's maternal grandfather was also a typical Irishman whom she admired as a child. Her mother Emily, was the second daughter in a large family. She was adopted by an Aunt who was proud of her roots that consisted of seven kings of France – the Milesian kings. Whenever her mother would be naughty as a child, her Aunt would look gravely from behind her spectacles and remind her that her behaviour was not worthy of a person belonging to the seven kings of France.

Emily would then cry in shame and shrink away from doing anything mean or petty.

This story about her mother's Aunt, came down to her through Emily, her mother. She put the same values into her only daughter Annie. Honour had to be upheld even if it meant enduring any amount of pain.

A brave front had to be kept before the world while taking pride in honour and one should rather die of starvation than run in debt.

Later Annie thought, perhaps the training her mother gave her was to come very useful in her public life when she was attacked with criticism and slander. It taught her to suffer with dignity and with self-respect.

Annie and her mother shared a very deep bond that grew stronger and stronger with time. She felt that her mother was the sweetest, tenderest, proudest and purest of women. Her mother served as an ideal of all that was noble and dear throughout her growing years. Her mother loved and protected her and her home was a beautiful place because of her.

Annie's family was a happy one, living in a house with a garden, situated at Grove Road. She was then three years of age. Their mother would serve them at the dinner table with her father and her brother who was two years older than her. She remembered her fourth birthday, and how she was jumping excitedly on her cot that day.

Annie's father was a doctor. He was well educated and had mastered many languages - French, German, Italian, Spanish and Portugese. He would often sit and read out passages from ancient and modern literature. He loved to read aloud for her mother who listened while she worked. He was a liberal and had outgrown orthodox beliefs. Her father and her mother were very loving companions.

But the happiness of Annie Besant's family did not last long. Once, during the dissection of the body of a person who had died of consumption, her father cut his finger. One surgeon suggested to him to amputate his finger but others laughed it off, saying, nature should not be tampered with.

In 1852, in the month of August, he got a severe cold after riding on the top of an omnibus in wet weather. The cold settled on his chest and an eminent doctor, after examining him declared that he would not live more than six weeks.

On hearing the news, her mother simply fell on the floor like stone. Soon she overcame her agony and served her husband day and night, lovingly, till he passed away.

A day before his death, Annie was taken to say her good bye to her father. He told her to be a good girl always and to listen to her mother. Just three days back, Annie had celebrated her birthday. Her father had gifted her a doll. She had named her Cherry. She insisted her father to kiss Cherry.

The next day on October 5, her father died. Her mother broke down and locked herself up in her room the whole night. After a lot of insistence, she opened the door in the morning. All were amazed to see that her glossy black hair had turned completely grey in that night because of grief.

As a child, Annie was imaginative and religious. Her dreams and visions were also an important feature that marked her childhood. She even treated her dolls as living, she loved stories of fairies and elves and even believed in them. The flowers and pet animals were not objects but were treated gently and caressed. Her playthings would also come alive in her playful fancy.

After her father's death, the period of struggle started. Her mother's anxiety was tremendous as they had no money to fall back on. She had never seen any problems when her husband was alive. Being a doctor, he earned a good living.

In a move to help her mother, two of Annie's father's relatives offered to educate her son. But Emily had wanted the best possible education for her son. Many relatives did not agree with the young widow's foolish pride which she upheld, in such a penniless state! But she had a firm mind and she educated her son at Harrow, where the fees was not so high and then decided to send him either to Oxford or Cambridge. Her father's relatives, Western and William Wood, remained her friends and did support her in the early part of her struggle.

During one of her family visits nearby, she met a lady who took her on her lap and talked to her. Later she asked Annie's mother if she could take her and educate her together with her niece. Annie would of course come home regularly for holidays.

At first her mother refused as she could not imagine a moment away from her beloved daughter. Annie too was always clinging to her mother. But her mother realised that a good education was very important so she yielded to the request of this lady, Miss Marryat, who was the favourite sister of Captain Marryat, the famous novelist.

Miss Marryat took great delight in teaching the children. She would seek out and help to educate those children free who were pressed by poverty. The children called her 'Auntie'. She made learning a very enjoyable experience.

When the lessons were over, they would have fun going for long walks, rides on a pony and picnics in the lovely country around Charmouth. During holidays, Annie would go home to their dear old home and garden and show her good report of progress to her proud mother.

In 1861, Miss Marryat asked permission to take Annie with her on her trip abroad. For a few months before leaving they were given classes in German to prepare them for the visit to that country. They had already been trained to speak some French.

When in Paris, they visited all the beautiful churches and galleries of the Louvere where they became familiar with the masterpieces of art collected from different lands.

The picture galleries filled with the Madonnas and Saints and the exquisite music and the fragrance of incense in the churches brought her immense joy. Her imagination and dreams became more vivid.

After 1862, Miss Marryat was gradually training Annie to be more self-reliant and so Annie was no longer under her constant supervision. Miss Marryat said that now Annie was old enough to do things herself and should not get too dependent on her.

For the next two-three years, life was smooth for Annie. The mornings and afternoons were spent studying herself and the evenings were spent going for walks and rides and going to parties.

Annie's mother let no burden of anxiety fall on her dear daughter and even spoiled her. She gave her only joy though she herself was struggling to pay for her brother's school and college education. Yet, she never let Annie experience want.

Annie's chief companions at that time were the Fathers of the early Christian Church, and she spent her time reading and spending a devotional life. She fasted and to serve Christ was becoming a definite aim together with active service. She idolized only two persons. One was her mother, and the other was Christ.

In the Easter of 1866, she was introduced to the clergyman she married. A little mission church had been opened in a very poor district of Clapham. She, together with an Aunt decorated it with spring flowers, prim roses and violets enthusiastically. The poor children who crowded around to see were excited.

Here, she met Rev. Frank Besant a young Cambrigeman who was serving the mission church as deacon.

In the summer of 1866 she was engaged to him and in the winter of 1867 she was married.

The shielded life she was given and the way she was protected from all anxiety in childhood did not at all prepare her for womanhood. She was ignorant of all life's duties and burdens. This too became the cause of an unhappy marriage.

From the very beginning Annie and her husband were an ill – matched pair. He had very high ideas about the husband being a figure of authority and the wife being a figure of submissiveness.

Annie was used to her freedom. She was impulsive and hot tempered with total indifference to home details regarding its management.

In 1868, Annie took up writing. She wrote some short stories and sent to the 'Family Herald.' When the cheque came she was delighted because that was her first earning. It gave her a sense of independence.

In January 1869, her son was born. Annie then devoted more of her time looking after the baby, than on reading and writing.

In August 1870 she gave birth to a baby girl. She was a delicate child because her birth had been premature. In 1871, both her children were ill and down with whooping cough. Since her daughter was very young her lungs were badly congested and doctors felt that her recovery would not be possible. Annie was distressed as she loved her children passionately. But she fought Death for her child.

The child finally recovered but those weeks of anguish left a deep impression on Annie's mind.

Mr. Lauriston Winterbotham, the doctor who treated and cured her children also remained one of Annie's kindest friends in her married life.

Once when her daughter's condition became stable, Annie collapsed with weakness and could not get out of bed for nearly a week, When she looked back upon the pain and agony she had faced in the past months, she started losing faith in religion. She was transforming into an atheist and her personal belief in Christ also changed. How could a good God tolerate pain and evil in the world she questioned.

She saw the suffering of the poor, the state of her mother, whom she dearly loved, and how she had been defrauded by a lawyer she trusted, how she ran into debt, her own cheerful life turned into a bondage and now the torture of the tiny innocent baby. All these events disillusioned her.

She started to question the dogmas of the Church. This sense of outrage she felt, made her lose faith in Christianity. She became a rebel against the churches and finally a non – believer in God.

Giving up belief in God meant to give up Christianity. But Annie's husband was a clergyman and what would be the result of it all? She had to prepare for another kind of outer warfare. She stayed away from the Communion and that led to gossip and if she continued in this way Mr. Besant's professional and social life were both being put in danger.

In 1873, she was told that she had to conform and to attend the Communion or she had to face exclusion from home. She chose to leave her home. Her mother was heart broken.

Annie had paid a heavy price for her freedom and now she had to make her own future. Her first job was as a governess, which enabled her to support her children and her ageing mother.

In 1874, she decided to join the Free Thought Society. They encouraged their members to voice their opinion and thoughts in the meetings that were held regularly. Women were taught to be brave and to become financially independent. During these lectures she met many educationists and people from other professions. She became interested in Hinduism and started to study the life of lord Krishna. She was so impressed by the mystic world of the East, that she started learning Hindi, hoping to visit India someday.

During this period, she came in touch with Charles Bradlaugh, a famous man in London, who drew great crowds whenever he spoke on social and economic issues. He was a free thinker. At their very first meeting, both Annie and he talked, debated and got along very well together. For many years they worked together and carried the Free- Thought movement forward. Annie so well grasped the ideas of the movement and even improved upon them, that Bradlaugh soon insisted that Annie also lecture herself. She turned out to be an intensely magnetic orator. She became an outstanding public figure by the wonderful charm of her speeches. She denounced religious intolerance.

Charles Bradlaugh was editor of the radical National Reformer and leader of the secular movement in Britain. Bradlaugh gave Annie a job working for the National Reformer and during the next few years she wrote many articles on issues such as marriage and women's rights.

In 1877, Annie Besant and Charles Bradlaugh decided to publish The Fruits of Philosophy, Charles Knowlton's book advocating birth control. They had to struggle against orthodox opponents. Even though the book was enormously popular, the two were charged under "obscenity" laws. They had published material that was likely "to deprave or corrupt those whose minds are open to immoral influences."

Besant and Bradlaugh were both brought to trial but later acquitted. Both of them had personally made their defence and not employed any counsel. This prompted the opening of the world's first birth control clinic one year later in the Netherlands.

It was at this time that her husband moved the court to take her little daughter away from her. He felt Annie was an "unfit" person because of her ideas. Annie rose to her defence, and argued her case point by point. She lost the custody of her child and was deeply grieved. Determined to regain custody, she learnt the laws of England and became the first British woman to defend herself. She won the case and received much attention.

As for the children, the moment they were old enough, they came back to her and remained great admirers of their mother. They even shared her views on nature and the destiny of man and joined the Theosophical Society.

George Bernard Shaw, attended some of her lectures and considered Annie Besant to be the most brilliant orator of the century. It was after meeting him that she joined the Fabian Society, where socialist ideas prevailed. She worked for children's and women's rights and she was the secretary of the trade union formed to help the girl's who were working in match factories.

Annie was asked to review "Secret Doctrine" by the editor of the Review Of Reviews. The moment she read the work, something within her mind flashed. She wanted to interview its author Madame Blavatsky. She became Madame Blavatsky's disciple because from the moment she met her, life for her changed. She separated from her secular friends and became firm in her resolve to serve the world. Working for humanity remained her sole passion. In 1891, after Blavatsky passed away, Annie Besant took over the leadership of the Society. With her developmental work she developed it all over the world, opening branches all over Europe, America, Canada, Australia and New Zealand.

The Theosophical Society had shifted its major activities from England to India around 1879. On November 16th 1893, Annie was offered an opportunity to go to India. She was delighted as she had for so long wanted to visit this ancient land that was now under British rule. England she felt was barbaric and India was civilised. A few years back she had already taken up the cause of India's independence in a pamphlet with the title, 'England, India and Afghanistan.'

She came as stranger but she managed to change the religious life of so many Hindus. She was well read in the Hindu philosophies and her knowledge amazed the people. Her love for India poured in every speech and many Indians listening to her almost wept with emotion when she gave them hope of a great new India.

Annie Besant lived like the people of India, she ate vegetarian Indian meals on large green leaves instead of plates, wore simple plain saris and kept hardly any furniture in her house. She called India her 'motherland.' Whenever she landed in Bombay and saw the faces of Indians, she felt as though she was with her own people. She spoke out fiercely against the British rulers.

She founded the Central Hindu College in Benaras, in the year 1898. Theosophists from the United States and Britain came to help her in the work of the college. Dr. A. Richardson was made its first principal. He was succeeded by Dr. George S. Arundale, who later became the International President of the Theosophical Society after Mrs. Besant passed away.

In her activities for the cause of education, Dr. Besant was supported by many noblemen and Indian princes. As a recognition of her services for education in India, she was conferred upon with the degree of Doctor of Letters.

Annie Besant also organised a movement called ' The Sons and Daughters of India.' For children, she started the 'Golden Chain' movement that is active in Scotland, Spain, U.S.A. and many countries of South America.

In the year 1918, she organized the Indian Boy Scout movement. Though the boys obeyed the Scout Law they sang Indian songs and wore Indian turbans. When Lord Baden Powell visited India, his movement and Dr. Besant's movement were merged and she was made 'Honorary Scout Commissioner for India.'

Annie Besant tried to reform some old Hindu customs like child marriage and sati. She felt that the people should not marry their daughters before the age of sixteen.

Along with Raja Ram Mohan Roy and other leaders she fought till sati was banned by law. She absolutely condemned this practice of the burning of wives on the funeral pyre of their husband.

After their husband's death women were socially made outcasts and were kept away from auspicious occasions like weddings and other such joyous ceremonies. Their heads were shaved off and they were considered the cause of their husband's death. Annie did not agree with this treatment of widows and spoke out against custom.

Since all human beings are equal before God she also raised her voice against untouchability and ill treatment of the lower class.

In 1913, Annie Besant entered politics. She started a weekly newspaper called 'The Commonwealth, in January 1914. Just a few years later she purchased the Madras Standard and in August she changed it's name to New India.

She stood up for the cause of the Indian National Movement and wanted Home Rule for the Indians.

As a politician, her first work was to bring together the two sections of the Indian National Congress which had been divided at Surat in 1907. One was represented by Mr. G. K. Gokhale and the other by Mr.B.G. Tilak. There were some basic differences in their opinion but Annie Besant, with her efforts brought the two groups together on a common platform of the All India Home Rule League.

The journalists in India were taught by her to write strong and forceful articles based on facts, criticising the government actions and yet to keep their protests within the law. This method was followed by the London Times.

The British became suspicious of her activities and tried to curb them. They disliked the fact that a foreigner was getting together with the Indians and was even a part of the Quit India Movement. They threatened to stop the publication of her paper. They stopped her entry into Bombay and in 1917, they arrested her and put her in jail.

The news spread and protests and processions were carried out not only in India, but also by people abroad, demanding that she be released from jail. By the force of the tremendous reaction generated by this arrest the British were compelled to release her.

As soon as she was released, her popularity rose so high that she was elected the President of the Indian National Congress which met in December.

When Mahatma Gandhi launched his Non Cooperation Movement against the British she disagreed with him, even though she held him in high regard. She believed in "passive resistance." One part of Gandhiji's campaign was the breaking of certain laws, which were to be announced to the people in a bid to put pressure on the government. Annie Besant felt breaking of any general law was not correct and she openly challenged Gandhiji's policies.

This shocked the people of India because Gandhiji was highly loved by Indians. Many friends withdrew support because of her remarks and members of the Home Rule also turned against her.

Deeply hurt, she decided to return to England and fight India's cause from there. She made one last effort to force the British to accept the demand for Dominion Status by drafting the outlines of a bill for the Dominion of India before the British Government. Though the initiative was taken, it did not get much support from the members of the British Parliament.

Annie Besant passed away peacefully at her home in Adayar on September 20, 1933. Though she did not live to see India get her freedom, she was content with the work she did for the country. She said she had no regrets as she had done her best for India's freedom.

In most of the three hundred or so writings, Annie Besant conveyed her deep understanding of the laws of nature. She was also a mystic. In 1906, she , in one of her speeches, envisioned that a day would dawn, when, throughout the length and breadth of India, brotherly cooperation would prevail and the young as well as the old would work towards the regeneration of the Motherland.

This was the kind of hope she gave. This was the kind of immense love she idealised. Perhaps this was another of her search in the name of Truth. After all Truth was what she followed, as we learnt from her own line that is inscribed on her tomb.

⌘ ❖ ⌘

HELEN KELLER

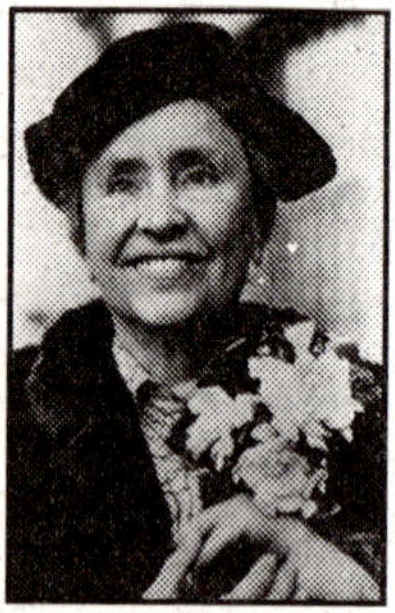

Helen Keller's name symbolizes the courage of an indomitable spirit. The story of her life comes alive to every reader belonging to just about any generation. Her pain and isolation bridges the gap between the deaf and blind Helen and her readers. She fought overwhelming odds and came across a winner; so her story gives hope to people who find themselves in hopeless situations. Even though she became blind and deaf, she dared to look destiny in the face and change what it had in store for her.

In a little town of northern Alabama was born Helen Keller in the year 1880 on the twenty seventh of June. The town was Tuscumbia. Her father Captain Arthur Henley Keller, was in the Confederate Army while his wife Kate Adams Keller was his second wife and hence was quite younger than her father.

The house they lived in was a simple, white, clapboard house built in 1820 where Helen lived for the first couple of years of her life. It was surrounded by a lot of foliage and completely covered with vines and climbing roses forming a sort of screen around the house. The trees all around the garden were home to humming birds and swarms of bees. Helen loved this simple old fashioned garden with violets and lilies and some very rare sweet flowers. She loved the fragrance of roses that hung down from her house and the feel of the leaves and the tender grass. All this gave her a kind of comfort that only nature can give.

Helen's father was the editor of a weekly local newspaper and owned a cotton plantation while her mother worked on the plantation and economized by making her own butter, lard, bacon and ham. Helen's father was very loving and indulgent. He was quite a storyteller and would spend quite some time with Helen, narrating witty anecdotes. He was devoted to his family and would often bring guests home, with people enjoying his hospitality. He would hold Helen's hand and lead her in the woods while she enjoyed the touch of trees and leaves. He died in 1896 after a short illness. This was to be Helen's first major loss.

Helen was born a healthy baby with full sight and hearing. She was given all the attention that first borns get in any family. Helen's mother wanted to name her baby Helen Everett after her own mother but her father had wanted to give her the name of Mildred Campbell, an ancestor on his side whom he respected a great deal. But eventually she was called Helen Adams.

As a six month old baby she was quite assertive and one day delighted everyone by saying, "Tea, tea, tea." The day she was a year old she took her first tiny steps leaping out of her mother's lap to run towards the moving shadows of the leaves. Soon she fell down and cried to be taken up again in her mother's lap as all babies do.

Three seasons later, when Helen was not yet two years old came that illness which changed her life forever. In the month of February she got a fever and doctors said it was acute congestion of the stomach and the brain. Early one morning when she was cured of the fever everyone at home was very happy but no one till then even suspected that she would never be able to see or hear then onwards.

Helen had memories of her illness and the soothing comfort of her mother's presence when she grew up. But later those memories dimmed and that illness was like a nightmare that left her world a dark and silent one.

After her illness, Helen became dependent on her mother and clung to her, following her around the house. She would touch and feel the objects around her. Gradually she learnt to communicate by nodding her head and gesturing with her hands. At the age of five she learnt to sort out and fold her own clothes from the laundry.

Martha Washington, her cook's daughter and Belle their dog, stayed with her most of the time. She could communicate with Martha quite well as she learnt her sign language.

They spent their time on small tasks like kneading dough in the kitchen, making ice cream or grinding coffee. She enjoyed feeding the tame hens and turkeys. The stable of the horses interested her and Martha as much as the milking of the cows in the morning as well as the evening.

Helen established fits of temper when she was unable to get what she wished. She would even bully Martha who would readily submit to whatever Helen wanted done. Even as a child Helen was strong willed and strong headed as she herself admitted in her autobiography. Helen was by then realizing that other persons were communicating by mere lip movement and not hand gestures. She tried to do the same but did not succeed. This would make her extremely angry and she would scream and kick in desperation for a long time.

Both the girls, Martha and Helen were fond of mischief. There were various incidents when Helen was particularly naughty as a child. An interesting incident was when she locked her mother in the pantry because she had newly learned how to use the key. Her poor mother remained locked inside for three hours before she could come out as the servants were in the other part of the house. All the while her mother was banging at the pantry door, Helen was sitting and laughing at her mother's plight. She could of course feel the vibrations caused by the banging. So naughty was she!

In fact it was her love for pranks that set her parents thinking. They felt they should arrange for a teacher for educating Helen before her mind got occupied in meaningless activities. But the problem was they lived very far from the school for the blind or the deaf so the possibility of someone coming to teach Helen in a small place like Tuscumbia, was very remote.

In Baltimore, there lived a famous oculist so her father thought of taking Helen to him hoping he would cure her as he had cured many difficult cases.

Full of hope, Helen was taken to Dr. Chisolm in Baltimore but they met with disappointment when he told them that he could not do anything for her eyes.

However they were advised to meet Dr. Alexander Graham Bell of Washington for further information about schools of deaf or blind children. The doctor felt there was no reason why Helen could not be educated.

Her father then decided to take her to Dr. Bell in Washington. This time though there was not much hope in his heart as he left for the journey. Disappointments saddened him but Helen traveled with childlike enthusiasm enjoying the excitement of such frequent travel.

Helen's first meeting with Dr. Alexander Graham Bell itself made her love the sympathetic way she was treated by him. Besides he seemed to understand her sign language. This was perhaps the beginning of a wonderful friendship between the two that resulted in the light of knowledge for her.

Dr. Bell suggested that Helen's father write his problem to Mr. Anagnos. He was the director of the Perkins Institution in Boston, where much was being done for the blind.

Helen's father wrote to Mr. Anagnos requesting him for a teacher who was qualified to teach a blind girl. Finally this time hope came to him in the form of a letter of assurance from Boston that a teacher was finally found for Helen. She was Anne Mansfield Sullivan. This was in the year 1886.

Just three months before her seventh birthday in the year 1887, Helen's teacher Miss Sullivan came to start her education. At that time Helen was absolutely unaware of the surprising turn her life would take from that moment onwards. The suffocation she felt at her inability to express herself often made her very angry. Her bursts of anger were a result of this desire to express herself which was not being fulfilled.

Miss Sullivan was of Irish immigrant stock and being a highly sensitive teacher she soon helped Helen to learn that every object had a name. Anne Sullivan was a fresh graduate and she had her own sight partially restored after an eye disease that nearly turned her blind. Perhaps that is why she succeeded with her specialized training in providing the handicapped Helen the relevant guidance. It was entirely her unfailing and repeated attempts that later made Helen Keller a legend all around the world.

The first thing her teacher did was to gift her a doll that was sent by the little blind children of the Perkins Institution. When she played with it Miss Sullivan took her hand and gently with her finger spelled the word 'd o l l' into her palm. Helen immediately got a desire to imitate this finger movement and rushed to her mother to do the same. She was of course simply imitating this movement in a child like manner without knowing she was actually learning words that would open a whole new world of communication for her.

Bit by bit Helen was finding expression for her emotions so she was a happier child than before. Anne Sullivan, on her part used firmness with love while teaching Helen. Though intelligent Helen had become quite undisciplined and indifferent in her behaviour towards others. Anne and her pupil moved into a small cottage on the land of the main house to try and get Helen to improve her behaviour. While at the table, she observed no table manners and would eat with her hands and from the plates of everyone at the table. Helen resorted to more and more temper tantrums whenever Anne attempted to teach her table manners or make her brush her own hair and button her shoes. Anne punished her student gently during these tantrums by refusing to talk to her through the language of spelling words on the palm.

Helen's behaviour did improve in the following weeks and a bond also developed between the two. With determination, her teacher spent hours each day teaching Helen the manual alphabet and trying to show Helen the importance of these finger symbols which till then she treated as an interesting game. It was not as simple a task as it sounds. Once while learning the words "mug" and "water", Helen was confused and couldn't differentiate between the two. Her teacher persisted in making her learn while Helen kept repeating the same mistake. Suddenly Helen was overcome with anger once again, she took her new doll and threw it on the floor, breaking it. Far from remorse she felt glad at having it.

Anne Sullivan knew she had to be patient so she gave Helen her hat to wear and both set out on a walk in the sunshine outside.

What happened during that walk is best expressed by Helen herself in her autography, 'The story of my life'.

"We walked down the path to the well-house attracted by the fragrance of the honey suckle with which it was covered. Someone was drawing water and my teacher placed my hand under the spout. As the cool stream gushed over one hand she spelled into the other the word 'water', first slowly, then rapidly. I stood still, my whole attention fixed upon the motions of her fingers. Suddenly I felt a misty consciousness as of something forgotten, a thrill of returning thought, and somehow the mystery of language was revealed to me. I knew then that "water" meant the wonderful cool something that was flowing over my hand. That living word awakened my soul, gave it light, hope, joy, set it free! There were barriers still, it is true, but barriers that could in time be swept away."

This made her realize that everything had a name. When she touched objects it gave her a new meaning and significance. A new thought process got triggered. That day she learnt words like father, sister and teacher.

When she reached home after that enlightening walk, she remembered the doll she broke in frustration. For once she felt sorrow and remorse as she picked up the pieces with tears in her eyes. This eventful day also brought new hope and she looked forward to the next day with her teacher.

Miss Sullivan would take Helen by her hand and take her across fields, and to the banks of the Tennessee River to show her the marvels of nature. There in the open sitting on the warm grass Helen learnt how the sun and the rain helping the growing of trees, and that the earth is round, and how food that we eat is grown. She learnt about birds and other creatures. Helen learnt to delight in the fragrance of the flowers that were there in the woods. She found beauty in these by merely feeling and touching them. She enjoyed spending hours in the lap of nature and dreaming sweet dreams.

The more she learnt, the more she wanted to know. With every step, a new world of information opened up before her. It was by all means a very painful process for a blind and deaf child who unlike other children could neither see nor hear the lip movements of others around her. So much of all this an average child with normal senses learns by mere observation.

Objects and their names after having being mastered the next step was grasping the meaning of abstract words like 'love' and 'think'. When one day she gave her teacher a few violets from the garden, Miss Sullivan spelled 'I love Helen' into her hand.

Helen could not understand what love was so her teacher pointed to her heart. Helen couldn't understand and asked if the sweetness of violets or the warm sunshine was love.

That day Helen was puzzled as to why her teacher was unable to show 'love' as she would show her other objects while teaching.

Once when she erred while stringing beads and tried to concentrate on the correct arrangement that Miss Sullivan touched her pupil's forehead and spelled the word 'THINK' carefully. In an instant Helen understood that the word 'think' was the name of this thought process going on in the mind. It was her first grasp of an abstract idea.

Later her teacher explained with simple words and with examples of clouds and flowers how one cannot touch love but can feel its sweetness and that love alone is the greatest source of happiness in life.

With this simple revelation, she felt a sense of oneness with other souls.

Learning to read was the next thing. With the help of cardboards which were printed with words in raised letters Helen started learning to read. With her innovative methods Miss Sullivan made learning more a kind of play than work. She never nagged Helen when she was unable to grasp or couldn't recall something.

In the month of May of the year 1888 Helen together with her mother and teacher went to visit Boston. At the Perkins Institution she met many other little children who were blind and immediately started making friends with them. They could understand her language and welcomed her warmly. It pained her a bit to realize that though blind, they could hear, a sense that was deprived to her. But she thoroughly enjoyed their company and days in Boston just flew by.

In Boston, she visited Bunker Hill and learnt the story of the brave men who fought on that spot. It was her first brush with the subject of History.

The next day she took her first visit to Plymouth by a steamboat. She enjoyed the motion but the sound of the engines frightened her and she began to cry thinking it was thunder.

She made many friends in Boston. One of them was Mr. William Endicott and his daughter. They even visited their beautiful farm at Beverly. He remained a good friend to her and it was because of her experiences with him that she named the city Boston –"the city of kind hearts."

When it was vacation time at Perkins Institution, during the summer it was decided that she go to Brewster with Mrs. Hopkins. Helen was longing to touch the sea and feel its wonder since she had read about the ocean in a book – "Our World." Once in her bathing suit, she ran across the warm sand to plunge into the sea. The motions of the waves that she experienced gave her a sense of thrill. But she did panic when she got tossed around by the waves and was thrown back to the shore. The fear of the playful nature of rough waves was gone when she was back safe in her teacher's arms on the shore. With an innocent child like curiosity she inquired "who put salt in the water?" after her first experience in sea water.

One of Laura Bridgman's teachers called Mrs. Lamson came to meet Helen Keller and told her about Ragnhild Kaata. She was a deaf and blind child like Helen but had been taught to speak. Helen was quite eager to learn to speak as she could make audible noises by keeping her hand on her throat and the other felt her lip movements. Before she lost her voice and sight, as a baby she was rapidly learning to talk but suddenly after her illness she wouldn't speak because she couldn't hear.

Her teacher took her to Miss Sarah Fuller who was the principal of the Horace Mann School. Miss Fuller decided to teach Helen herself and so in March 1890 she started learning to speak. In the course of eleven terms, Helen could speak short sentences that were broken and far from perfect but it gave her a sense of strength. She talked to her toys, birds and animals. It was as though the words she fingered on hands had suddenly got wings. She had to labour much and practice most of the time but she did it all longing one day to show her family what she had achieved.

That day did come when on the platform of Tuscumbia station her mother, father and little sister were overjoyed on hearing ever syllable that she uttered. Her mother hugged her in glee while Mildred her little sister took her hand and danced.

In March 1893, she went to Washington during the inauguration of President Cleveland. She went to Niagara and the World's fair with Dr. Alexander Graham Bell. Mr. Higinbotham, President of the World's Fair, allowed her to touch and feel the objects that were exhibited. Dr. Bell explained and described the objects everywhere she went and that trip became a great learning experience for her. With such interaction she leapt out of her fanciful world of toys into the real world of man and the progress he had made in his everyday life.

Before the end of 1893, Helen Keller had studied the histories of many countries like Rome, Greece and the United States. She learnt French and Latin grammar. She could recite passages from works of poetry that she had memorized.

In 1894, Miss Sullivan took Helen to the Wright – Humason School for the Deaf in New York city. She came to know about it while attending a meeting of the American Association to Promote the Teaching of Speech to the Deaf. The two years she spent in the school there taught and trained her in lip reading. She even studied Geography and Arithmetic in the school. The teachers there, Helen wrote, were always striving to help the children make the most of their natural tendencies. This planned attitude helped the disadvantaged children overcome the sense of oppression that surrounded them.

Helen Keller joined the Cambridge School for Young Ladies in October 1896. Miss Sullivan would attend classes with her and acted as interpreter. Miss Sullivan would also patiently spell into Helen's hand all the things that the teachers said. At the Cambridge School she got the pleasure of having the company of other girls. She would play games with them and go for long walks during which some girls learnt to speak to Helen so Miss Sullivan would not have to do so for her.

During Christmas her mother and sister spent their holidays with her. For six months Mildred stayed with her in Cambridge and studied there. Both helped each other in play as well as work.

Helen took her preliminary examination for Radcliffe in 1897. The list of nine subjects she offered were Elementary and Advanced German, French, Latin, English and Greek and Roman history. She passed in everything with "honours" in German and English.

During her second at school Helen had to face many difficulties. That year she had to study physics, algebra, geometry, astronomy, Greek and Latin. Many of the books she required had not been embossed for her in time and in the huge classrooms it was very difficult for her to get personal attention. Miss Sullivan had to finger all the books and lectures. A task that seemed impossible. She needed Braille writer to solve problems in mathematics.

Once when Helen was unwell and did not attend classes, Mr. Gilman thought she was unable to take the strain and changed her studies. But this would not enable Helen to give her final examinations with the rest of the class. Miss Sullivan and Mr. Gilman disagreed and ultimately Helen's mother decided to withdraw both her daughters from the Cambridge School.

A tutor of Cambridge, Mr. Merton S. Keith was arranged to teach Helen. He came to Wrentham twice a week and taught her algebra, geometry, Greek and Latin. Miss Sullivan as usual did the role of interpreter. Getting attention from her tutor, Helen was able to prepare for her college better and faster. He explained things patiently to her. Problems in mathematics she still found difficult but he helped to make learning it interesting.

In June 1899 she took her final examinations for Radcliffe College. Miss Sullivan was not allowed to read papers for her. Mr. Eugene C. Vining was told to copy the papers in American Braille. Helen had used only the English Braille for algebra and was dismayed by the American notation in the papers.

Her admission to college was a long struggle but her dream of going to college was fulfilled in 1900. At Radcliffe, what she missed most was leisure time to reflect or read what she loved most. There was a lot to study and she required more time than the other girls to prepare her lessons. Her subjects included economics, Elizabethan literature, Shakespeare and the History of Philosophy.

Helen Keller graduated with honours from Radcliffe in 1904.

Besides her love for books, Helen loved outdoor sports right from the time she was a little girl. She knew swimming and would often take her friends in her boat for a ride, rowing herself. Sailing and canoeing was also a source of enjoyment to her. When alone she would play the card game of Solitaire. Her playing cards were marked in the upper right hand corner with Braille symbols which indicate the value of the card.

On her experiences of things unseen she wrote a very telling explanation-"It seems to me that there is in each of us a capacity to comprehend the impressions and emotions which have been experienced by mankind from the beginning. Each individual has a subconscious memory of the green earth and murmuring waters, and blindness and deafness cannot rob him of this gift from past generations. This inherited capacity is a sort of sixth sense-a soul sense which sees, hears, feels, all in one."

"The Story of My Life" was Helen Keller's first book. It was published serially by the Ladies' Home Journal. This book contains her letter from 1887 to 1901, besides her early autobiography and comments by John Albert Macy. This book became an American classic. It is full of life and engrossing, besides being extremely useful for educating the deaf and blind. By her experiences, Helen contributes greatly to that knowledge which is needed to teach the deaf and blind. In it she describes the terrible isolation of those inflicted by this handicap.

In 1927, she published "My Religion" concerning her conversion to Swedenborgianism and in the year 1930 appeared the second volume of her autobiography entitled "Midstream".

Helen Keller's friends included many of the world's greatest people like Alexander Graham Bell, Mark Twain, William Dean Howells, Charlie Chaplin and Andrew Carnegie. She was received by nine presidents and bestowed honorary degrees upon her by half a dozen of the most prestigious universities in the world.

From 1924 onwards, being associated with The American Foundation for the Blind, she traveled extensively to all continents and to every state in America working for the possibilities of welfare for the handicapped. She campaigned actively because she felt she could serve humanity best by working on behalf of the blind and deaf. She was awarded the Presidential Medal of Freedom from Lyndon Johnson in 1964.

The blind and the deaf were earlier put in mental asylums but Helen's efforts put an end to this practice. She even informed the public about prevention of blindness of newborn babies through her articles in the Kansas City Star and Ladies' Home Journal. Helen and Anne gave lectures towards speaking of her experiences and beliefs to large crowds. Helen's talks were interpreted sentence by sentence by Miss Sullivan and were followed by question and answer sessions.

But by 1918, the demand for Helen's lectures had diminished so they toured with a more lighthearted vaudeville show which demonstrated Helen's first understanding of the word 'water'. These shows were hugely successful. At the same time they were also offered a chance to make a film in Hollywood called 'Deliverance', the story of Helen's life. But unfortunately, this film did not prove to be a financial success as they had hoped it to be. Helen and Anne made a good living from their lectures and by the question-answer sessions, they were earning up to two thousand dollars a week, which was an impressive amount of money at that time.

Helen and Anne settled outside Boston. In 1905, Anne married John Macy, an instructor from Harvard but this marriage did not interrupt the friendship with Helen. Macy had an influence on Helen and she became a militant socialist. Anne, Macy and Helen lived together in Wrentham, Massachusetts and during this time Helen wrote "The World I live in" revealing her thoughts to the world for the first time. In 1913, "Out of the Dark" was published. This was a series of essays on socialism. Helen's political views were now known to the people.

Helen's mother Kate died in 1921. The cause of her illness was not known so Helen was left with only Anne as her companion. That very year, Anne fell ill and the following year she got a severe bout of bronchitis which left her unable to speak aloud so she was unable to work with Helen on the stage anymore. John Macy left them in 1914, so a young Scotswoman by the name of Polly Thomson served them as a secretary-cum-house-keeper.

They also spent a lot of time touring the world and raising money for blind people. In 1931, they even met King George and Queen Mary at the Buckingham Palace, who were not to mention, quite deeply impressed by Helen's sense of touch. In 1932, John Macy died and Anne's health got worse. Anne Sullivan's blindness had recurred in the year 1930 and she finally died on 20th October, 1936. She had been a faithful and constant companion to Helen. She had helped Helen all through her school and college days. On her lecture tours, Anne accompanied Helen supporting her student to the very end as both shared a common concern for the handicapped. The people's indifference towards the handicapped was transformed by their efforts towards social reform.

In a book entitled "Teacher: Anne Sullivan Macy" (1955), Helen paid tribute to her dear teacher discussing the difficulties she faced while trying to teach Helen the language of communication.

After Sullivan died, Helen and Polly moved to Arcan Ridge, in Westport, Connecticut, which was a special house built for them by the American Foundation where Helen stayed for the rest of her life. Helen with the help of Polly, started traveling and resumed her life going on to become a familiar personality in Washington D.C. They travelled the world fund-raising for the American Foundation for the Overseas Blind. They visited Japan, Australia, South America, Europe and Africa.

During this time a fire destroyed their home at Arcan Ridge and the house had to be rebuilt. Among the things destroyed was Helen's latest book "Teacher".

Polly Thomson's health also began to deteriorate and she got a mild stroke during her visit to Japan. Doctors advised Polly to refrain from straining herself and after sometime Polly did recover. In 1953, a documentary film was made about Helen's life called "The Unconquered".

In 1960, Helen lost her second companion Polly and the following year, she herself became the victim of a stroke. Though she lived for another seven years, but they were years of loneliness. It was in 1957, that "The Miracle Worker" was first performed which was a drama portraying Sullivan's first success in communicating with Helen as a child. It was a live television play in the United States. It was written as a Broadway play in 1959, and it was a huge success and the actresses playing Anne and Helen both received Oscars for their performances.

Helen then started retiring from her public life because of the series of strokes she suffered. Sometime in this period of her life, she was elected to the Women's Hall of Fame at the New York's World Fair. On June 1, 1968, at Arcan Ridge, Helen Keller died peacefully in her sleep. She was cremated in Bridgeport, Connecticut and a funeral service was held at the National Cathedral in Washington D.C. where the urn containing her ashes was later deposited next to those of Anne Sullivan and Polly Thomson.

This place which is the final resting place of Helen is a popular tourist attraction and there is a bronze plaque erected with the following inscription written in Braille:

"Helen Keller and her beloved companion Anne Sullivan Macy are interred in the columbarium behind this chapel."

The plaque had to be replaced twice because it was visited and touched by so many people.

The essence of the remarkable life that Helen lived can best be summed up in Helen's own words:

"The public must learn that the blind man is neither genius nor a freak nor an idiot. He has a mind that can be educated, a hand which can be trained, ambitions which it is right for him to strive to realize, and it is the duty of the public to help him make the best of himself so that he can win light through work."

⌘ ❖ ⌘

MARIA MONTESSORI

Maria Montessori was the only child of Alessandro and Renilde. She was born on August 31, 1870 in the eastern part of Italy in a town called Chiaravalle, the same year

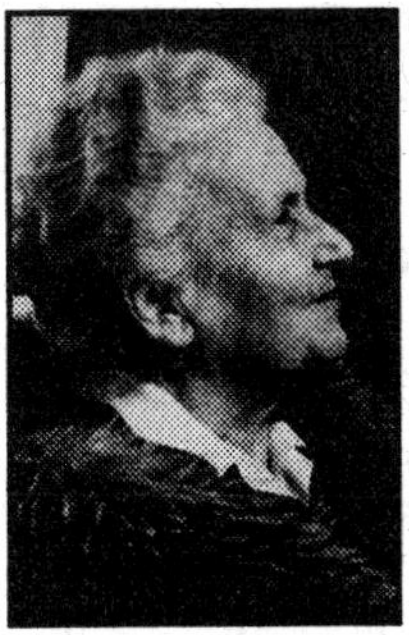

that Italy became a unified and free nation. Her father worked for the Italian government as an accountant and a member of the bourgeois civil service. The first few years of her life were spent in the small town of Chiaravalle but later when she was nearly five years old, the family shifted to Rome, where her schooling began.

In Italy, it was not uncommon to see children leave school after sometime, either to go to work or as in the case of girls, to get married. Only those students who were interested in pursuing a career, stayed back and specialised in subjects of their choice. Some girls learnt Greek and Latin with the aim of becoming teachers.

There was nothing very brilliant about Maria Montessori as a student. When she was a child, though she nursed dreams of becoming an engineer. In fact the teaching profession did not interest her at all then. She was however quite ambitious as a child, even of a dominating nature many thought and liked her for it while a few others despised this quality. But she did have a strong sense of duty from the very beginning.

Around the age of twelve, Maria's interest changed and she developed a keen urge to learn Mathematics. This was a subject that was chosen especially by boys, so there was no special school for girls. So to study mathematics, Maria had to attend a secondary school for boys. She could not go around and play and mix with the boys during free time but had to sit quietly in a room. Perhaps that was the school's way of keeping her safe from the boys, who were in a great majority.

She passed out of school with a good percentage and wanted to specialise also because the study of science and mathematics had by then sharpened her intelligence as well as interest. She wanted to go to a medical school. Her family totally disagreed, specially her father. As proud parents of an attractive girl, they wanted to get her married into a prestigious family. Even the mingling of boys and girls in Italy at that time was not permissible. Her parents were particularly careful to see Maria did not interact with any boy. A medical profession seemed an impossible choice for a girl.

Maria was insistent. Besides, bit by bit, both Alessandro and Renilde, Maria's mother and father, observed that their daughter was exceptional. She was already becoming well known by her public speaking and was developing a mind of her own. Seeing her determination her father gave his consent but there were strict rules that she had to obey. Keeping away from boys and not going or coming back from school without someone accompanying her.

Becoming a doctor was her only idea so she agreed to her father's conditions. But this was just the beginning of problems to come. Besides the lack of facilities for a girl student, the school was full of boys who at the slightest of opportunity, ridiculed her. They would trouble her in the classroom during the lectures also. Whatever anger she may have felt at such harassment, she kept to herself but she did feel isolated when she was not even allowed to participate in any discussions.

In a medical school dissection of the human anatomy is a regular feature as is the study of bone structure with the help of skeletons. Maria was not allowed to do so in the company of other boys and the school staff and authorities suggested that she do her work in the laboratory after all the boys had left for home. That meant Maria had to stay back alone and work with dead organs and tissues in the laboratory. She would shiver in fright, get repulsed by the sight and smell of the human bodies. At times she would even wonder whether it was the right profession for her.

At one point her father requested her to give it all up seeing how sick and feverish his daughter was becoming. Maria too felt she should inform her professors of her inability to continue her medical studies. Later it was her assertive spirit that urged her not to give in but continue on the course she had set for herself. She succeeded in her solitary struggle and by the age of twenty-six, she became the first woman to get a medical degree in all of Italy.

A word about Maria as a young girl now. Though she was determined and strong willed as a person, there was another side to her also. She loved dressing up well, taking pride in her hair styles and looking attractive. There was a gentler side to her that took an interest in homely chores like embroidery.

But Maria Montessori's experiences at school with the boys had developed within her a great concern for the rights of women. She felt instead of early marriages women should opt for a career if they so desired. She was different from the other women activists in her approach to men. She was softer and more reasonable and stood for a healthy kind of friendship between men and women.

It was no surprise when Maria was invited for a conference in Berlin to speak on the topic of equal pay to women and men for equal work. This was after she qualified for her medical degree. Women labouring in factories were paid a paltry sum as compared to men. Maria was a naturally emancipated woman and she spoke with ease and confidence. She instantly became famous and her speech was given a wide coverage. More and more journalists wanted to interview her and photograph her.

Maria did not let all this attention distract her from her real purpose in life. If she was speaking up for women she says, she should also do something. She then became involved with patients at the mental hospital and worked as an assistant there.

Children inflicted with mental illness were discarded by society and lived a locked-up life with no social care. Maria had read the works of two Frenchmen and the German Friedrich Froebel. Besides her concern for the mentally handicapped she also toyed with the idea of sending patients of mental hospitals to special schools. She also became a part of the activities of the National League for the Education of Retarded Children.

The two Frenchmen by the names of Jean Itard and Edouard Seguin had specialised in the education of the deaf and mentally retarded children. They felt the condition of the handicapped could be improved by exercises aimed at the improvement of their senses. Then there was a German named Friedrich Froebel who was the founder of schools for children up to the age of seven. Maria studied the works of these men in great detail with the idea of developing their research further.

Her interest in the education of children was growing even though she worked as an assistant doctor in the mental hospital. Besides her regular job she treated women and children privately in her clinic. At the age of twenty-nine she was appointed director of a school for the mentally handicapped in Rome. For two years she worked at this job that was offered to her.

Maria Montessori was gradually being recognized because of her lectures on education which she gave extensively in many parts of the world. She was loved by her audiences as well as by the press. Her magnetic personality and scholarly approach impressed a wide audience. She traveled to distant countries alone and that was yet another act of boldness by a young lady and Maria by doing so, exhibited another aspect of her adventurous nature. It was also her link to the events and happenings of the rest of the world.

Maria was becoming the symbol of the new woman and lost no chance to lecture and prove that women were no less in any way. You can imagine what her reaction was when an eminent scientist declared that women were inferior to men because their brain contained less phosphorous than men!

The answer to such ridiculous claims Maria felt was to educate women. To refute such arguments women needed intelligence through education and not mere emotionalism. Only then would men take notice of women as equal beings and grant them the freedom to pursue other activities.

After observing the learning abilities of the mentally deficient Maria Montessori focussed her work on the learning patterns of normal children. After considerable research and study she found the educational systems wanting. She saw the child as a unique being who was an admirable individual and who had to be unconditionally accepted since he was a product of life's beautiful expression. The health and nutrition of children also decided their performance and there was never any need to force them as they had an innate desire to learn. The right environment and the right materials were important to help them become free thinking and independent children.

By careful observations of the development stages she proved her concepts when in two years time some of her "deficient" students were able to pass standard tests for Italian School Children. Her efforts were praised and greatly recognized but she felt if her methods were applied instead of the traditional methods in all public schools the results would be far better still. The government did not permit her so she concentrated on the care of poor children.

On the personal side of her story, Maria Montessori while working for the mentally handicapped children met Guiseppe Montesano who was a colleague there. The two of them fell in love. The affair was a closely kept secret between family and friends and Maria never spoke of it publicly. In 1898 Montessori's only child, a son, named Mario Montessori was born. The father's identity was kept a secret as it was quite shameful to have a baby outside marriage. Guiseppe Montesano betrayed Maria and married some other lady later. Her baby was of course sent to live with another family and later educated in a boarding school. Till then he did not know who his real mother was. Amazingly the people came to know the truth about her son only after her death when her will was read out. He was during his mother's lifetime always described as her nephew even when he worked with her as her Chief Assistant.

The new problems that got created for Maria when her son was born and also because she was deserted in love resulted in her giving up her post as director in Rome. Surprisingly now she turned her attention towards teaching, something that she disliked as a child. She returned to the university to learn the methods of teaching, psychology and also hygiene.

When she was thirty five years of age she was made in charge of a training course at the university of Rome. Her refreshing approach in her lectures caused a lot of excitement among the trainee teachers. They loved to attend her classes that were lively and inspiring. It was a direct contrast from the stiff and sober approach prevalent those days.

The classroom scene in the nineteenth century was one of rigid conformity. Seated in rows, the children were asked to repeat back whatever the teachers said. Small wonder then that the children would lose interest by the daily dull procedures of learning. Many would avoid going to school or simply resort to pranks in the classroom. The teachers in their turn were not at all student friendly but believed in training the brats with physical punishment. Schools with such a dreary atmosphere were hardly a pleasure but a place more like a prison.

When Maria Montessori was thirty seven years old she had already become quite famous in Italy not only as a doctor but also as an activist and a lecturer. But the work she started in the educational field, specially for young children made her a well admired pioneer all over the world.

Her desire was getting stronger and stronger to modernize the system of education so she decided upon giving up of her university chair and her medical practice both to work with a group of sixty young children, of working parents in the San Lorenzo district of Rome. This opening of the first Children's Home was the first step that revolutionized the education of children. It changed the way adults viewed children and understood them.

Maria saw that if children were given a neat and orderly place to learn and work they take pride in learning. She got carpenters to build child sized school desks and chairs so that children could be seated comfortably. They did not have to sit and learn in one place only. She created seating areas on the floor, complete with rugs and cushions. The children were not taught but simply looked after while they found activities to absorb them. Maria had ordered sets of learning materials, which were later known as the "didactic apparatus" and were so designed that children could try again if they went wrong till they could do the task correctly.

The daily looking after and running of the Children's House was done by Candida Nuccitelli who was the caretaker's daughter.

Maria Montessori had named the Children's Home – Casa dei Bambini. She wanted the school to be very different and unlike regular schools of those times. By modifications in the classroom Maria revealed to the entire world qualities in children that were much higher than what adults understood. When given enough freedom in a specially prepared environment. She showed how four or five years old learnt to write and read spontaneously, who chose to work rather than go to play or eat sweets, loved silence, concentrated well, helped each other and managed well without adult help, were also obedient and not wild and unruly.

Not only in Italy but in other parts of the world children were never treated with such a great degree of respect. Adults were often reprimanding them most of the time. Montessori also created a game of silence, "somewhat like meditation," where each child was able to start the day with a sense of peace.

The children of San Lorenzo that came were poor children of slums totally neglected by society ad by home. While their parents went to work they were left to roam about outside the home till the evening. So the owners of the apartments decided to pay someone for these urchins to be looked after during the daytime. With the success of the first Casa within a few months itself Maria was requested to open another one for the children staying in the next block. Gradually in other parts of the city even richer parents were requesting Maria to set up Casa for their children. One Casa was opened in Milan in 1908.

Maria would get a lot of visitors who would see her revolutionary methods. Articles were written about her methods in newspapers and magazines. A rich Italian nobleman, Baron Leopoldo Franchelti and his wife helped Maria in her efforts and became friends with her. Baroness Franchelti also convinced Maria to write a book on her lectures. The book, The Montessori

Method was published in 1910 and later translated in more than a dozen languages.

Children liked freedom of choice, yet their actions were orderly. Reward and punishment, she wrote in the book was not helpful in their learning as they were naturally inclined to be well behaved. Some of her observations about little children were so different from what was already known about children that many were filled with disbelief. Specially when she said that the children at the Casa had refused the sweets offered to them. Maria also told people that children loved silence which no one was ready to agree with. But she would take the people to her Children's House and prove the above two observations were a fact.

Maria Montessori devised sets of boards with alphabets glued on top of them at the very basic level. She spent a considerable amount of time making experimental sets which she first tried again and again at her Casa. She would continue till she got the correct one for that age group of children. The materials were attractively coloured and shaped in geometrical patterns and they were easy to handle.

Four years after opening of the first Children's House, in 1911, her method of teaching had become a world wide movement with many state schools in not only Italy but Switzerland, India, China, Mexico and Korea also approving this Montessori System. Not just the poor but rich parents also thought it best to educate their children in Montessori Schools.

A leading magazine in America came to know of her work and carried on articles at length with photographs about Maria Montessori, her schools and the apparatus they used. The response from the public was tremendous. Readers in America became curious and many wanted to join her training programmes to improve the already existing schools. By the end of that very year the very first Montessori School had opened in the United States that was run by an American teacher who was first trained in Rome by Maria. The number of schools multiplied into a hundred very soon only in the United States.

Maria toured America in 1913 and spoke in Boston, New York, Washington and many more places. She was welcomed and her lecture halls would be packed with people. She did this as many people had made a business of using her name for their own purpose.

During her second visit to America she took part in the World Exhibition, held in San Francisco. Here she put on exhibit a Casa made of glass walls. This transparency helped people see the procedure conducted inside. It caused quite a lot of excitement among the people. She was a far sighted lady in more ways than one.

But with growing popularity and growing number of schools came the question of management. Maria was burdened with a lot of work as she would not hand over the control to any other person. Running a world wide network of schools from Rome was not possible. So the movement in America broke up while fresh new ideas came up. Toys and games were manufactured for children using the Montessori name. Trainee teachers would find it difficult to go to Rome to learn. Maria too was unable to go back to America.

Maria had her share of critics too. Though initially people absorbed Maria's methods because of it's novel approach, they felt she attributed too many holy qualities to the child. She, in her instructions was laying down lists of detailed activities that included teaching children how to blow their own noses and the type and amount of food to be eaten everyday. These details many people found difficult to accept. Then disagreements would often creep up between Maria and her disciples because many of them wanted to add fresh ideas to modernize it still more. Having been a science student Maria's methods were quite scientific too. In fact too much so that some remarked that education was not just matching colours and shapes. Maria on her part ignored criticism and concentrated in her schools where students and parents were both needy to accept her teaching methods.

In 1922 when Mussolini took over the government in Italy, Maria was made Chief Inspector of schools throughout Italy.

She also got aid in the form of money for her schools. But Mussolini being a dictator wanted his country's children to be well versed with the techniques of war. He wanted them to have a particular uniform and join the Fascist Youth Organisation. Maria did not agree to let her schools be a part of this organisation. As a result, instantly all Montessori schools in Italy were closed down. Maria decided to leave the country and go and live in Spain.

By the time she was sixty her son Mario had also joined her in her school work. But in Spain a civil war broke out and once again a dictator started ruling. With advancing age she thought it right to settle in one country with her son and grandchildren. But there was much anguish in her personal life too. Mario her son was actually introduced to the world as her nephew. Mario's marriage also broke up and he was separated from his wife. He worked with Maria acting as her interpreter during her lecture tours. Maria usually lectured in Italian, her mother tongue.

She wrote two more books – 'The Secret of Childhood' and 'The Absorbent Mind.' After leaving Spain she settled in Holland for two years from 1937-1939. In the year 1939 she left for India.

Age had not affected the alertness of Maria's mind or love for new places and people. The people of India welcomed her warmly and respected her ideas and philosophy. She stayed in India for six years. The enthusiasm people showed in India made her visit here a very pleasant and enjoyable one.

After her six year stay in India she went back to Holland than came to India in 1947, toured Pakistan in 1949 and then lectured in Europe. She kept herself constantly busy with her tours and lectures. She died in the year 1952 in the month of May, at the age of eighty one in Noordwijk, Holland.

The many souvenirs Maria Montessori received, together with her medals, her diplomas, photographs with friends and leaders were all displayed at Koninginneweg, Amsterdam, her last home. It is used as Montessori Association office now.

Dr. Montessori's work will last as long as there are children in this world. She understood them well, loved them and helped them grow with keen and eager minds. The soul of the child and its great potential was the essential point of all her movements. She widened the concept of education to include an absolute new kind of interaction between the pupil and the teacher. She broke away clearly from the stringent traditional roles. Through her lectures she even influenced men and women to modify and modernize their roles in society.

Dr. Maria Montessori, the woman who began a revolution in the field of education, changed the way we think about children more than anyone else had done. In "Education for a New World", she says:

"Scientific observation has established that education is not what the teacher gives; education is a natural process spontaneously carried out by the human individual, and is acquired not by listening to words but by experiences upon the environment. The task of the teacher becomes that of preparing a series of motives of cultural activity, spread over a specially prepared environment, and then refraining from obtrusive interference. Human teachers can only help the great work that is being done, as servants help the master. Doing so, they will be witnesses to the unfolding of the human soul and to the rising of a New Man who will not be a victim of events, but will have the clarity of vision to direct and shape the future of human society."

In another excerpt, from her book, "The Absorbent Mind", we come to know how important a link the infant was for her at all levels of civilization. Infancy is a period of true importance, because, when we want to infuse new ideas, to modify or better the habits and customs of a people, to breathe new vigour into its national traits, we must use the child as our vehicle; for little can be accomplished with adults. If we really aspire to better things, at spreading the light of civilization more widely in a given populace, it is to the children we must turn to achieve these ends.

⌘ ❖ ⌘

INDIRA GANDHI

Indira Gandhi's name becomes a symbol for women. A potent symbol that has come to stay. She headed the world's largest democracy – India. A country known for its tradition and one, that organized a massive struggle to free itself from British rule.

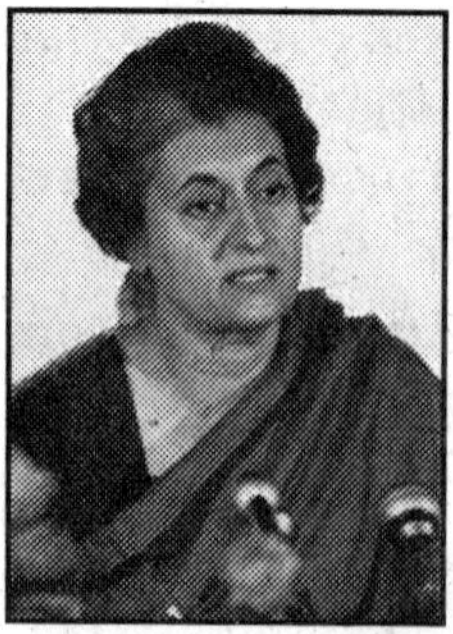

The job of Prime Minister was a complex one but her fierce passion for her country was simple. In her biography, Pupul Jayakar writes of her – "She was no democrat but she loved her country with passion and tenderness. Like a tigress guarding her cubs, her antennae would awake at the slightest threat. She never ceased to regard herself as a guardian of India and its frontiers.

Her courage was epic. She dared, refused to be intimidated whatever the odds."

The roots of such passion can be traced to her as this is what Indira had to say of herself – "From the age of three I felt responsible for myself. Whether I was or not, did not matter, I also felt fiercely responsible for my parents, for I felt they were defenceless and relations and friends took advantage of their goodness. I had a feeling of wanting to protect something very big. My earliest memories are of a feeling that there was a debt I owed; I could never explain to whom or for what, but it was a debt that I had to repay."

Ironically, the great leader, Indira Priyadarshini was born in the year of the Russian revolution i.e. 1917. The month was November, the date nineteenth and the city was Allahabad.

Besides her father Jawaharlal and grandparents Motilal Nehru and Swaroop Rani, there were in the verandah many uncles and aunts all waiting anxiously and expectantly for the birth of a baby boy while Kamla, Indira's mother laboured in a room near the courtyard.

Out of all these, the happiest was her father Jawaharlal Nehru at the news that a baby girl was born. She was named Indira after the name Indirarani that belonged to her grandfather Motilal Nehru's mother. A strong, resolute and brave lady was Indirarani. So I guess Indira did not just inherit a name but a legacy of fine grit and guts! Thus a foundation of future greatness was laid.

Indira was born in an illustrious family. Her grandfather Motilal Nehru, was an astute lawyer whose fame had had spread in the entire province. Because of his sharp mind and deft arguments, people from the aristocratic families would come to him for legal advice or approach him to fight their cases. To add to his charm was the fact that he was a handsome and well dressed man with a good amount of grace.

As his practice flourished, he decided to move his family into a new mansion that he named 'Ananda Bhavan.' The house had forty-two rooms and the life style and furniture in it reflected a strong British influence. Although for his wife Swaroop Rani he did have a part of the house that was Indian in ambience. It was a huge joint family that got his warmth but his word of authority was final. A condition he lay for all at home was that English had to be the spoken language at home!

Jawaharlal, Motilal Nehru's son was born on 14th November 1889. He took great pride and interest in his son. When Jawahar was about twelve years of age his father employed Ferdinand Brooks as a tutor for him. Brooks educated and trained the boy well for further education in England. At the age of fourteen Jawahar was escorted by his parents to be admitted to Harrow. Later he went to Trinity College at Cambridge.

Meanwhile Motilal rose in affluence and acquired a lavish lifestyle playing host to the likes of British Commissioners and Governors. Though he had strong Western leanings, when it came to the choice of a girl of his son he was a conservative Kashmiri Brahmin. Kamala, Indira's mother was a beautiful girl from Delhi's Atal Kaul family. She was not so highly educated nor was she fluent in the English language and the ways of the British. Before the marriage Kamala spent a few months at a relative's place in Allahabad where a governess Miss Hooper acquainted her with the ways of the western life style prevalent in the Nehru household. This idea was of course Motilal's.

The wedding ceremony of Kamala and Jawahar took place on 8th February 1916. Needless to say the wedding celebrations were on a grand scale.

After marriage things were hardly smooth for Kamala. She had to adjust not just to her husband Jawahar but to the entire Nehru household. For one, there was Vijayalaxmi who was Nehru's younger sister and nearly of the same age as Kamala. A pretty girl who was brought up with love and admiration. She was extremely fond of her elder brother Jawahar and often went riding with him or accompanied him to parties and social gatherings. Being possessive of her handsome brother it was natural that she resented Kamala's entry into the family. She did not want to share her brother's attention with anyone let alone Kamala who already seemed a misfit for the Nehru household in the eyes of Vijayalaxmi.

Then Swaroop Rani was no easy mother-in-law to get along with. While the mother-in-law could get annoyed and difficult Kamala could get stubborn like a sixteen year old that she was. Very often she would sit and cry at the sad plight. Her husband Jawahar too had been brought up in an atmosphere alien to her and she took tome to mature to his twenty seven years of age as compared to her just sixteen. There were innumerable other relatives in the house whose dispositions she had to get used to. As it was Jawahar spent a good deal of his time conversing and riding together with his sisters.

This was the state of her mother and the household at the time Indira was born. Events outside the house were no different. The Rowlatt Act was passed and Mahatma Gandhi had reacted by forming Satyagraha Sabhas. Jawahar had seen Gandhiji and he wanted to join the Satyagraha movement. Moreover Jawahar felt it was time to change his father's outlook so that he too would join him in this confrontation with the British. Motilal was aghast at his son's suggestions and his sudden change of attitude. The arguments generated in the house caused a lot of tense moments. Indira was barely two years of age but vividly remembered the facial expressions and behaviour of all elders, with the typical sensitivity of a child. That was one time she saw her mother's face radiant and glowing. Perhaps Kamala was proud of her husband's decision. It was during this time that the home 'Anand Bhavan' started becoming the hub of activity with varied people visiting it regularly.

Motilal thought it best to resolve things by visiting the Mahatma's residence where they talked for several hours. Gandhiji too advised Jawahar not to act in haste.

To protest against the Rowlatt Act huge crowds gathered in many parts of India. There were ten thousand or so people gathered at Jallianwala Bagh on the day of Baisakhi – the spring festival. General Dyer, in a bid to teach the Indians a lesson ordered his soldiers to fire on the helpless men and women present in the park. This massacre of innocents greatly enraged even the most liberal of Indians, prominent among them was Motilal Nehru who was absolutely furious. He gave up his practice and burned all his foreign goods and clothes and even discontinued his youngest daughter Krishna's education at the Convent. His lifestyle immediately became a direct contrast to the earlier western one and he together with his son opted for a simple and austere life. Mahatma Gandhi's call for Satyagraha was reciprocated by many professionals from the field of law and education and a considerable amount of young students, all of whom readily went to jail.

When Indira was about five years of age she was presented a small charkha by her grandfather Motilal Nehru. She even learnt to spin on it. She even organized a Bal Charkha Sangh where other young children also learnt to spin and weave. Mahatma Gandhi's influence was present on all members of the Nehru family and Indira was among the youngest entrants to his call.

The childhood graph of Indira was far from stable. Not surprising as the country was in a state of turmoil and since both her father and grandfather were actively involved in the political struggle her routine was greatly affected.

When her father and grandfather were jailed she would spend a lonely time with her mother for company. Other times their house Ananda Bhavan became a meeting point for Freedom fighters where her father and grandfather would be busy in discussions. She would often breeze in and out of the room or sit on their laps to get their attention. Most of the time she was quite indulged by her grandfather and fed her favourite pastries but sometimes she was chided for disturbing the serious meetings. The house was a huge one, so she had plenty of space indoors and outdoors to run around and play as she wished.

It was in the lawns around Ananda Bhavan that Jawahar taught his daughter to walk and run. He too would gently run along with her, while the daughter would do so on her toes instead on her heels. A habit which continued with her into adulthood. Swift and brisk strides with the weight on toes – that was her walk. She said she had learnt to breathe with her heels.

Whenever Jawahar was not in jail, he and Kamala would ensure Indira had dinner with them to compensate the time spent away from her. After dinner she would climb up the stairs to go to her own room. Though she pretended to be brave then, later on in life she admitted being quite afraid of the dark in her room.

She spent a considerable amount of time in the garden, sometime climbing up trees for fun and sometimes to curl up in some hollow of the bark to read her favourite story books. Somehow the greenery around the house energised her so she liked to play around the trees under the open sky. Her dress was mostly a kurta pyjama of Khadi, topped with a cap quite often. So the garden became a sort of a haven for her and tree tops, a cozy place to relax when in need of solitude. Perhaps it was her method of getting away from the chaos of the huge household.

Even when alone in her room Indira loved to play with her dolls often enacting the freedom struggle that was such a familiar site for her those days. Other time she would imagine herself in the roles of Joan of Arc and Jhansi of Rani and picture herself leading the people bravely.

Aware of her isolated childhood Jawahar Lal Nehru, her father, when in prison wrote informative and educative letters to his daughter about India and its wonderful history. Indira enjoyed reading those letters in her room.

"They helped me to see things in perspective and I never saw an Indian problem merely as an Indian problem but as an international one. These letters were to be published under the title 'Letters of a Father to a Daughter.' I don't think he was consciously trying to form my mind, but he was bubbling over with interest in things that it just split out."

In 1924, Kamala had given birth prematurely to a son but he didn't survive more than a few days. So Indira remained the only child of her parents. But in the Motilal household this news came as a great disappointment. Kamala's health was gradually suffering and she was turning weak. There wasn't much support emotionally from her in-laws and neither the required attention of her husband. Indira though a child sensed her mother's plight and inwardly felt a surge of anger and rebellion. To protect her mother, she would often react boldly but soon saw that it had little impact. Later to check her elder's behaviour she would maintain a long silence to cover the seething anger within. This way of responding helped her mother more.

Meanwhile the doctors diagnosed tuberculosis as the reason for her mother's ill health and so she was admitted for several months in a hospital in Lucknow. So Indira had to shuttle between Allahabad and Lucknow. She enjoyed spending her time with her grandmother and her uncle in Lucknow.

Her uncle (mother's younger brother) was a science student and had collected samples of various plants and insects including snakes! Indira of course soon adapted to the new surroundings and adored all the attention they gave her. .

There was no improvement in her mother Kamala's treatment at Lucknow so it was decided to shift her to Switzerland. Indira with her family left for Genovia in the March of 1926. They took up a flat at 46, Boulevarde de Tranche and Indira started to go to school. She became fluent in the French

Language. Jawahar would personally drop her and fetch her back from school but later decided to let her venture on her own in a bid to teach his daughter self-reliance early in life.

Schooling was exciting there with plenty of project work that took her back to nature. An exercise she enjoyed thoroughly was collecting leaves and observing the scenic surroundings. Her father was visited upon by the great scientist Albert Einstein and Jawahar also paid a visit to the famous philosopher Romain Rolland. On both occasions Indira was with him as part of the subtle grooming her father was giving her.

Her mother Kamala was shifted to a sanitarium in Montana as her condition showed no improvement. Indira had to consequently change school and go to L' Ecole Nouvelle at Bex where she was admitted as a boarder. When her mother's condition improved they visited London and Paris and went sight seeing. Indira was taken to all places of historical interest and to the theatre also where she saw St. Joan being enacted.

They were back in India by the end of that year and schooling abroad had made her bold and to question things instead of accepting meekly. Her father gave her more time and attention. He instilled within her a love of books and very often she was presented books that she found difficult to understand, for example, H.G. Wells. She was too happy and content with her fairy tales but her father insisted upon her reading some good authors. At Allahabad she was admitted at the Jesus and Mary Convent. She was quite irregular in her attendance at school being away travelling with her grandfather or mother at hill stations. The students and nuns would often get critical of her and her family's political views so gradually she started losing interest in the school and decided upon leaving it altogether.

The atrocities of the police had made even the women folk of the Motilal household aggressive and active. They organized and addressed public meetings at street corners and persuaded others of their kin to become bold and face the British. Even lathi charges did not deter them. Indira accompanied her mother, aunts and grandmother in these processions acutely insecure as to what turn the events would take everyday. It was indeed a very unusual childhood.

Kamala's organisational skills and enthusiasm to lead defiant crowds surprised the men in the house. In jail, her husband felt admiration and pride for his wife who suddenly seemed to have transformed into a different person when encountered with hostile situations. In one of his letters to his daughter her wrote – "You are fortunate in being witness to this great struggle for freedom that is going on in this country. You are also fortunate in having a brave and wonderful woman for your Mummie, and if you are ever in doubt or trouble you cannot have a better friend."

Feroze Gandhi, a Parsee youth from a middle class family in one of her meetings had saved Kamala from the police lathi charge. Though he was arrested and beaten up by the police he continued supporting Kamala and often visited Ananda Bhavan. His family of course severely disapproved all of this.

When Indira announced her decision to stop schooling at the convent, her father arranged for tutors and arranged scholars to teach his daughter at home. He was observing that the ongoing freedom struggle had energised the little girl. She was becoming rebellious and decisive. She would be quick to give first aid to the injured at Swaraj Bhavan. She wanted to become a member of the Congress but was refused membership. Undeterred she formed her army of monkeys – the Vanar Sena, consisting of children between the ages of five and eighteen. These children worked as volunteers, nursed the wounded and delivered messages, etc. to the Congressmen in hiding. Indira of course was the head and controlling authority.

Her grandfather was tremendously amused and wrote out a suggestion which did not amuse his granddaughter one bit.

"I suggest the wearing of a tail by every member, size of it should be in proportion to the rank of the warrior."

Much like other children, she had to be cajoled into drinking milk. Once at home, she won a banana eating competition. She wanted to learn Urdu and was allowed to do so. But her father insisted she learn Sanskrit also even though Indira felt it was a dead language. The time Jawaharlal Nehru had for his daughter was scarce but whenever he had the opportunity he would wholeheartedly spend it in answering queries of her little mind. Sessions which she found quite enjoyable because they were undisturbed and totally hers.

Once at Ananda Bhavan when she and her mother were busy reading Tennyson's poetry a phone call came informing that Kamala would be arrested the next day. The two of them were alone in the house and with her mother gone she would be left all to herself. Kamala anxiously made arrangements for her daughter and future action of the congressmen. Kamala had at last proved herself worthy of the Nehru household and Indira too saw it as a great moment of victory for her mother. But Kamala felt confident that her daughter could take care of herself till she came back from prison. For the mother of a girl entering teens it was no easy task so Kamala wrote to her daughter from jail regularly to keep in touch of her routine activities.

The death of Motilal Nehru in1930 in Lucknow deeply grieved not only his son Jawahar but also his granddaughter Indira. The indulgent grandfather whose laugh had filled not just Ananda Bhavan but also filled young India's spirit with a sense of security was no more. She wept bitterly behind a pillar alone.

Jawahar took Kamala and Indira for a two week trip to Ceylon after his father's death which is in new Sri Lanka. They visited the Buddhist viharas and met the monks there and spent a relaxed fortnight after a very exhaustive time back home. Once back in their home city Jawahar plunged back in his political wo-k while tensions brewed again between the possessive Vijaylakshmi and thirteen year old Indira.

With Jawahar courting frequent arrests and Kamala's health deteriorating something had to be done about Indira's education. Mahatma Gandhi advised that she be sent to Pune to join the People's Own School. Separation from her mother at this young age distressed her. The students at the Pune school did all their work and classes were held under the shade of trees. There was not much space nor was there the privacy of her own room. She masked her grief, shock and anger. But her nature alternated between aggressiveness and reticence. When Gandhiji was held prisoner in Yeravada jail in Poona, Indira would visit him. He was now akin to an elder of their family, "whom I went with difficulties and problems which he heard with the grave seriousness which was due to the large eyed, solemn child I was." Gandhiji's patience amazed her. She stayed the whole day with Bapu when he fasted and saw him get weaker and weaker.

Rabindranath Tagore, the poet whose Shantiniketan was famous for it's cultural education was the next place Indira was sent to. Here she got accustomed to the company of other girls and learnt more about India's heritage. The campus had painters, writers, artists and musicians, the presence of whom inspired Indira's artistic inclinations. Here also the students cooked the food and cleaned the floor themselves and attended the early morning chants.

It was during this time that Feroze Gandhi had proposed to her but she had refused saying she had no intention of getting married to anyone as freedom of the country was uppermost in her mind.

In March 1936 her stay in Shantiniketan ended as she had to accompany her ailing mother to Europe for further treatment. In Berlin, Kamala underwent surgery but she developed a fever so she was shifted to a sanitarium, close to the Swiss border. Indira meanwhile set out for Switzerland in the hope of getting admission in her old school at Bex. School life she found quite oppressive though she became an expert at the ski lessons she took. This sport caught her fancy and gave her some cheerful moments from the anxiety over her mother's frail health.

Indira's mother Kamala finally died at a fairly young age on the 28th of February. Kamala was cremated at Lausanne. Just a day earlier Indira had spent time with her mother. The grief she felt at her mother's loss stayed with her forever. The eighteen year old Indira was left behind in Europe by her father to complete her education. She did find it difficult to mould herself as the typical British school girl at the Badminton School near Bristoland her experiences there were not altogether happy.

It was during her stay at Oxford that she became close to Feroze and they often would discuss her mother Kamala and her mental anguish. That seemed to be a great binding factor as Feroze had also worked closely with Kamala, and knew her well.

Education for Indira was interrupted once more when she went along with her father for a European tour. It broadened her outlook but made her very well. She had lost weight and her illness was diagnosed as pleurisy. She was homesick and wanted to return to India.

Feroze had travelled with her on the same ship and it was at this time that they decided to marry. Jawahar did not approve of this match as he felt Indira was still quite young and also because Feroze was a Parsee and Indira was a Hindu. Gandhiji supported Indira when she adamantly stuck to her decision. Her father too then gave his consent and they were married in 1942. Their son Rajiv was born in 1944 and two years later their second son Sanjay was born. They were both actively participating in activities against the British and were imprisoned for doing so. India became independent on the midnight of 14th August 1947. Jawaharlal Nehru became the first Prime Minister of India. The division of India distressed Gandhiji as communal riots broke out. Indira would visit the riot torn areas and also visit Gandhiji everyday. Peace returned but on January 30th 1948 Gandhiji was assassinated. He had been a great guiding source for India.

When Nehru started rebuilding the country, Indira together with her children moved to Teen Murti House, the official residence of the Prime Minister. She played the official hostess and went with him on his visits to China, Poland, Egypt and the Soviet Union. Her involvement in her father's work was total. She attended the conference of Asian and African countries in Bandung. She formed a womens wing of the Congress and campaigned for her party during the general elections. Soon she was elected as the chairwoman of the Allahabad Congress

Committee because of her hardwork. In 1960 she resigned from the post following the demise of her husband. Their's was a very turbulent marriage because both Indira and Feroze were strong willed persons.

The Chinese aggression was a big blow to Jawahar as he had worked towards having good relations with the neighbouring countries.

Nehru died on May 27th 1964, leaving the entire nation mourning at the loss of a great leader.

After her father's death, Indira continued her work for the country. She served as Minister for Information and Broadcasting in the cabinet of Lal Bahadur Shastri. After his sudden death she was installed as Prime Minister.

Immediately she strove to make her party popular but she had to face many challenges. The Indo-Pakistan war in 1971 won her a reputation of a courageous woman but it drained the country's resources. A shortage of grains ensued as rains were scanty. In the following elections she won by a very thin margin. There was dissent within the Congress so she split the party to solve the problem of her opponents.

Tackling the country's problems she abolished feudal practices and saw that land was distributed equally among the farmers. In the 1971 General Elections she won a landslide victory. In the second tenure the refugee problem ensued as a result of the civil war in East Pakistan. People fled from there to come to India. She even sent the Indian Army to East Pakistan and within a span of 12 days she won victory over the Pakistani forces. The world took note of this woman as a powerful leader and a good director of war. After independence, East Pakistan came to be known as Bangladesh.

Her declaration of a state of emergency in 1975 set a controversy rolling. Her younger son Sanjay became the leader of the Youth Congress and participated in political activities. The state of Emergency was put to an end and elections declared in 1977. The Congress Party lost the elections and Moraji Desai of the Janata Party became the next Prime Minister of India.

She had erred in her political judgement but within three years she came back overcoming personal and political odds and thereby proving her toughness ana single mindedness to all concerned.

Her son Sanjay's foray into politics was a short one. He died in a plane crash and that personal loss left Indira quite shocked and distressed. This time she turned towards her pilot son Rajiv who was married to an Italian girl Sonia. Rajiv gave up his job and entered politics, a field totally alien to him as he was a relatively simple and candid man.

In 1981 she took a firm decision and sent the army inside the Golden Temple to capture the terrorists. Sikh sentiments were hurt and some turned vengeful. On the fateful morning of 31st October 1984 she was shot by two of her Sikh bodyguards. Sonia her daughter-in-law immediately rushed her to the hospital. Rajiv was in West Bengal. With the news of her death, riots broke out in the country. Rajiv, her son was sworn in as the Prime Minister.

Shakthi Sthal is the name given to her resting place in Delhi.

Indira Gandhi tried to strive like her father did to free India and to see it advance in all spheres. Her dedication to her country was complete. In brief she was a woman of courage and dynamism.

Jawaharlal Nehru, in one of his letters to his daughter, had explained the two kinds of problem children – one was the spoilt child and the other was the neglected child. The blend of the two was what the world saw as the adult Indira Gandhi.

⌘ ❖ ⌘

MARIE CURIE

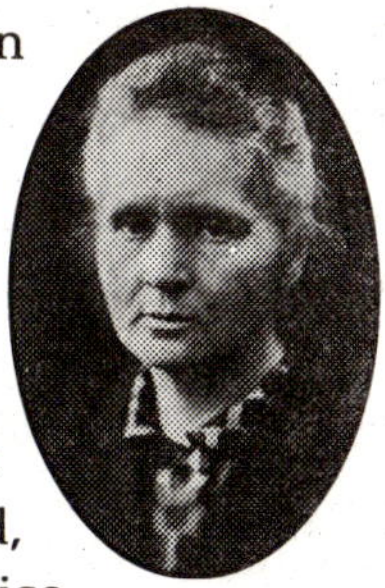

A brief introduction of Marie Curie would probably be as the woman scientist who discovered radium, or as a double Nobel laureate. But a study of her life in detail reveals the many aspects of her personality that she rounded off very well. She was, of course, an outstanding woman, both as a wife and as a mother, a meticulous scientist, a great patriot whose pursuit of truth took her to a foreign land, so she resolved to put all her strength at the service of her adopted country – France.

In the capital city of Poland was born Marya Sklowdowska, on the seventh of November, of the year 1867. She was called Manya affectionately by her family and friends.

Warsaw, the city of her birth, was in that part of Poland that was controlled by the Czar. It was not an independent country. Her parents, Bronislawa and Vladislav Sklodowski, had five children. Four daughters, named Zofia, Bronislawa, Helena and Marya and one son Jozef. Marya was the youngest amongst them. Both her parents were in the profession of education. Marya's father was a teacher while her mother worked as a headmistress in a privately owned girl's school, not very far from where they lived.

Patriots in Poland inwardly resolved to one day regain control of their nation, while the Russian authorities hoped to fully stamp out the language and culture of the polish people. The Russian supervisors had severely restricted the study of history too, but Marya's parents did their very best as educators to overcome these hurdles.

After Marya's birth, her mother resigned from her post as head of the school and the family moved to a boy's high school where her father was a maths and physics teacher. He earned a good salary but soon the Russian supervisor feared Vladislav would probably teach his students a great deal about Polish

6

culture. Sensing his strong sentiments towards Poland, the Russian supervisor fired her father who was then without a job and had very little money.

While her father was forced into lower academic positions, the family was also consequently forced into smaller and smaller homes because of the economic struggle that faced them directly.

On the prevailing situation, these were Marie Curie's own words:

"Constantly held in suspicion and spied upon, the children knew that a single conversation in Polish, or an imprudent word, might seriously harm, not only themselves, but also their families."

Nurturing them economically well may not have been feasible for her father but emotionally and intellectually he nurtured and encouraged them very well. On weekends he would read classic literature and poetry to his children. At home he even had a scientific apparatus that was earlier used to teach Physics. The Russian authorities had removed even laboratory work from the school curriculum.

All his efforts did bear fruit. Marya loved science and it was something she shared with her father. There was always ready help from him. Marya studied hard and soon she was the star pupil in her class.

In her memoirs, Marya's sister Helena writes: "I can still see little Maninsa (Marya), a plump girl with fair, curly hair bound up with a black velvet ribbon, wearing her apron trimmed with flounces; her eyes were a pale grey and they looked at the world with a smile, kindness and unusual seriousness. Although the youngest, she influenced her classmates with her unusual intelligence, abilities and great memory...."

Marya was barely eight years old when her eldest sister caught typhus and died. Three years later, tragedy struck again when her mother died of tuberculosis at the age of 42. The remaining members of the family were deeply grieved and depressed but drew closer to each other. Now, there was her father, brother Jozef and sisters Bronya and Helena.

Though struck by personal grief, Marya worked hard to achieve academic excellence. In 1883 she succeeded and was awarded a gold medal at her high school graduation. Though she was elated, the thought of having to shake hands with the Grandmaster of education in Russian Poland was not appealing to her. She was fifteen years old at the time of graduation and it was during this time that Marya suffered a nervous collapse and her father thought it best to send his daughter to spend a carefree year with her cousins in the country.

In 1885, after a refreshingly long holiday, Marya returned to Warsaw. She wanted to go in for an advanced degree like her brother Jozef, who was enrolled in the medical school at the Warsaw University. Since women could not do so, both Marya and Bronya attended the Floating University with their other friends. This was actually a women's club with 1000 ladies as members, who met to attend lectures by famous Polish writers and scientists. The fear of arrest was always there, as the Russians would have banned these gathering immediately. But Marya thought this was her way to utilize her spare time and stay in touch with other intelligent women. Being an illegal night school, they changed locations for every meeting to evade the suspicions of the ever-watchful eyes of the Russian authorities. This quest for self-knowledge was just the tip of the iceberg where the student's goal was concerned. They raised hopes of eventful freedom for their country – Poland.

The curriculum was nothing compared to Universities, but it did make them progressive and aware of developments in science.

Marie Curie described it as "one of those groups of Polish youths who believed that the hope of their country lay in a great effort to develop the intellectual and moral strength of the nation, we agreed among ourselves to give evening courses, each one teaching what he knew best."

Responsibility came quite easily to Marya. Lack of finance stopped both she and her sister Bronya from going abroad to the famous Sorbonne University in Paris. So, in 1885, Marya and Bronya thought out a plan, rather a pact. Bronya would go to the University while Marya, who was still not seventeen years of age, would work as a tutor and save money for her elder sister's education and living expenses. Once Bronya qualified and got a job, she would support Marya's education. Marya took this deal seriously and worked against all odds to shoulder this responsibility.

For two years Marya taught various subjects to children from wealthy families. But the saving from these was not enough.

So for the next three years she worked as a governess of the Zorawski family. She had to look after their two youngest daughters, Audzia and Bronka. Marya's job was difficult and she did not seem to be enjoying it. She continued nevertheless, as this was the only way she could realize her dream of being educated abroad.

Meanwhile, Marya read works on literature and sociology, besides books on physics and chemistry. She took up a correspondence course with her father in maths and chemistry lessons from a chemist in the beet sugar factory.

During this time, when she worked in isolation, it became clearer to her that maths and physics were her real preferences. So she undertook serious preparation with a determination to pursue her work in the future. Laboratory experience was till lacking because of the ban imposed by the Czar. Help came from her cousin Joseph Boguski, who was a former assistant of Russian chemist Dmitri Mendeleev. The Museum of Industry and Agriculture where her cousin worked was in effect a laboratory that trained Polish scientists. It was there that Marya was given a chemistry course by one of her cousin's colleagues on Sundays and evenings. Many a time she would try to manage the experiments on her own, often unsuccessfully too.

Sklodowski, her father, had by then become the Director of a reform school. Being better paid. He could afford to support Bronya's expenses in Paris. He even started keeping aside some money for Marya's studies and gradually it dawned upon her that by 1891 she would have enough money to start her studies in the famous University of Sorbonne in Paris. So her dream was finally becoming a realist in the month of November, 1891.

Eventually the day arrived when, after a forty-hour train journey, Marya came to Paris. Separation from her family and her country Poland, both of whom she loved dearly, saddened her. But there was a new life ahead that promised excitement and a whole lot of freedom. Under Russian rule in her own Poland, she had lived under severe restrictions. But in Paris she experienced a sense of freedom that was even greater than her French counterparts! French women those days had to be accompanied by chaperons wherever they went. Marya enjoyed her newfound freedom. The first thing she did was to change the spelling of her name from Marya to the French version Marie. This was when she enrolled at the Sorbonne University in Paris.

When in Paris, she first lived with her sister and brother-in-law. At the medical school, Bronya had met a Polish boy by the name of Casmir Dluski. The two had fallen in love and got married. Casimir was a patriot and was actively involved with the Polish exile community. Marya felt she too would have to regularly participate in such activities if she stayed with her sister and brother-in-law. She wanted to concentrate on her studies as she had a lot of catching up to do. Her father too advised her to be cautious and not jeopardize her future prospects. After all, he had suffered because of his pro-Polish sentiments and did not want his daughter to undergo the same fate in her profession. There was a second reason too. As Bronya's house was an hour's drive from the University Marie had to spend a lot precious time commuting. So after a few months Marie moved to the Latin Quarter that was closer to the University. It was a cheap, unfurnished room at the top of a six-story building of flats, giving her a wonderful view of Paris. It was cold at the top and she managed with a few basics like a stove to cook simple meals. She may not have had much material comforts but the two things she got in abundance were freedom and time and peace to work hard at her studies.

Marie was one of the twenty-three women studying science at the University where there were a total of 1825 students. It was an exceptional achievement for a girl student to get enrolled since Sorbonne was a very prestigious University. Reforms in

France were aimed at raising the standard of science so new classrooms and laboratories were constructed and only the most brilliant of scientists were chosen to be employed as professors in the University. Gabriel Lippman, the great physicist of that age who even won a Nobel Prize in 1908 for his work on color photography, had taught Marie.

Marie was happy that she was finally in the place of her choice, but she also realized that her fellow students were far ahead of her in technical excellence. Her background of science and maths was not enough. She spared no time and effort and plunged wholeheartedly into her studies. Dark circles would form around her eyes and she would faint with hunger but her focus was always on studies. Yet of her situation all she had to say was ".....my situation was not exceptional, it was the familiar experience of many of the Polish students whom I knew...."

In the summer of 1893, all the hard work she had put in was rewarded. Marie stood first in her Master's Degree physics course and in the following year she got the second position in maths. Seeing her outstanding abilities, some senior French scientists used influence to award Marie a scholarship reserved for an exceptional Polish student. The Society for Encouragement of National Industry had commissioned her to do a study relating magnetic properties of different steels to their chemical composition. For this project, she required a laboratory where she could start her work.

Marie's quest for a laboratory brought her face to face with a man called Pierre Curie. Little did anyone know that he would be Marie's partner not only in marriage, but also professionally the two would work together to change the course of science.

A word about Pierre Curie now. He was already known by people in the scientific circles for his experiments on magnetism and was Laboratory Chief at the Municipal School of Industrial Physics and Chemistry in Paris. He was a colleague of Marie's Polish friend, who was also a physicist. Pierre too belonged to a family that was poor but valued education. His father as well as grandfather were doctors.

He, alongside his brother Jacques, had done most of his studies at home. He was not paid very handsomely and he lived a simple life with his parents. He was thirty-five years of age then and was quiet, serious and completely dedicated to the cause of science. He felt women of genius were rare and had absolutely given up hope of ever finding a female companion to share his life and love of science.

But things were destined otherwise. Both Marie and Pierre were impressed by each other from the very first meeting. Marie loved his simplicity and his gentle smile that she felt inspired confidence. Pierre, on the other hand, felt Marie was different from the kind of women he had met earlier. In Marie was a devotion to the cause of science that seemed to match his own passion for the subject. They worked together and emotionally drew closer till gradually both of them felt it right to become life companions.

Marie wanted to complete not only her own doctorate but also wished Pierre would write up his research on magnetism. Though he had done important research, he had never completed a doctorate. In March 1895, Pierre was awarded the degree and soon afterwards he was promoted as a professor. The honor, of course, brought high salary benefits too.

In July 1895, after a year's courtship, Pierre and Marie became husband and wife. The wedding was a simple ceremony held on the outskirts of Paris where Pierre's family lived. Her father and sister Helena, came to Paris to specially attend the wedding. They did not exchange rings now was their any religious service. Pierre's family were non-practising Protestants. Marie's mother was a devout Roman Catholic, but her death so early in life and made Marie lose faith. In fact, there was no traditional bridal gown. Instead Marie wore a dark blue outfit which for many years later she used as a laboratory garment while working there!

The honeymoon was in Brittany where the couple merrily cycled on their new bicycles! Cycling was even then the perfect way to keep fit. Long hours of working indoors in the laboratory made life quite routine and monotonous. So Marie and Pierre would often use their cycles as a mode of relaxation and go for trips in the French countryside.

Their families helped them to set up a small home. Marie cooked and did most of the housework herself. Once again she shouldered her responsibilities of home and marriage very well. Perhaps at the very outset of life she learnt to do so sincerely when she worked as a governess to support her elder sister's education.

Marie wanted to teach science to young women so she decided to earn a certificate that would permit her to do so. She, of course, continued to work on her research on the magnetic properties of steel. She was allowed by the Director of Municipal School of Industrial Physics and Chemistry to work on the school premises. The school did not give her any financial aid and some metallurgical companies promised her fine steel samples for her research.

Another interesting fact about Marie's life is that out of the payment she received after submitting the results of her research to the Society for the Encouragement of National Industry, she gave a part of it to pay off the scholarship money she was awarded years ago. She too, in return, wanted to help some deserving Polish student. The reason she gave was "......having grown up in an atmosphere of patriotism kept alive by the oppression of Poland, I wished, like many other young people of my country, to contribute my effort towards the conservation of our national spirit."

To add to the happiness of the Curie household, a baby girl was born in September 1897. The child was delivered by none other than Pierre's own father, a physician himself. The baby was named Irene and was a great source of joy to the family. In years to come, Irene too proved her brilliance by getting many awards for research work.

Marie enjoyed motherhood as much as she enjoyed studying. She was an efficient manager of her home. Whether it was the household budget or keeping record of her daughter's development, both were done carefully. There was indeed never any doubt that she was equally good as a mother and as a scientist. Being part of an extended family had its benefits. Irene was looked after by her grandfather while Marie completed her lab work. He proved to be an excellent baby-sitter. This also sowed the seeds of a very close bond between the grandfather and grand daughter that was to forge in the years to come.

Although well occupied in her busy schedule with warm family ties to back her up, Marie missed her own family too. More so, as her sister Bronya and her husband returned to Poland.

Marie was now looking for a topic to do her doctoral research. A German physicist called Wilhelm Routgen discovered X-Rays in 1895 and by January 1896, X-Rays were being used in hospitals. The nineteenth century was characterized by great discoveries like electricity, telephone, photography and the invention of motor car. Scientists all over the world were striving towards improving the conditions of life. Any new invention would catch the attention of other scientists. Marie Curie too wondered to what other use X-Rays could be put. Antoine Henri Becquerel discovered that Uranium gave off similar rays. Marie wanted to investigate these rays. In that age Uranium was largely used as a coloring agent while glazing pottery.

In 1897, Marie started her work on Uranium in cramped storerooms and with very little money for equipment. She used the word "radioactive" to describe any material that gave off what she called emissions. She worked long hours testing other materials. Her husband Pierre was also taking an active interest in his wife's work. In 1898 Marie found that pitchblende produced greater emissions than Uranium. This proved that it contained elements that were more radioactive than Uranium. Pitchblende had to be broken down to isolate and extract the ingredients. It had to be boiled and stirred for hours before the liquid was electrolyzed and small amounts of the radioactive elements were isolated.

It was not an easy task but Marie persisted even though her back would pain with the long hours of stirring.

In 1898 they succeeded in extracting one of the radioactive elements. This is what Marie and Pierre wrote in their laboratory workbook:

"We thus believe that the substance we have extracted from pitchblende contained a metal never known before......If the existence of this metal is confirmed, we propose to call it polonium, after the name of the country of origin of one of us."

So they named it polonium, after Marie's homeland Poland.

But besides polonium, there was another, more radioactive element in pitchblende. Marie wanted to discover that. This process of extraction took four years before they discovered radium. Out of tons of pitchblende, only a fractional gram of radium could be isolated. Marie did not give up and in July 1902, her perseverance was rewarded and she finally told the world of their discovery. The blue light and heat that radium gave off fascinated other scientists. The Curies were generous and mailed out samples to other scientists.

Barely a few months before she succeeded in isolating pure radium, Marie's father died. She was filled with grief. The very next year she experienced a miscarriage and a little while later her sister Bronya's second child died of tubercular meningitis. Even her husband Pierre was suffering from ill health. Sometimes he would keep awake all night, weak and moaning.

In the year 1903, a letter from the Swedish Academy in Stockholm revealed that Marie and Pierre, together with Henri Becquerel, had won the Nobel Prize for Physics. Initially Marie was not nominated for her first Nobel Prize. Perhaps the male dominated scientific world wanted to ignore the work done by a woman scientist. Other scientists on the nomination committee intervened and Marie Curie's nomination in 1902 was validated for 1903.

Ill health prevented the Curies from going to Sweden to accept the prize. But newspapers were full of this extraordinary couple. Their flat was plagued with journalists and photographers and the Curies felt it was too much of an intrusion on their privacy. They were quite used to a quiet and simple lifestyle.

The prize money they received was used for poor students, besides their own families. Some of it went in the renovation of their flat and of course it was a great help in improving the lab conditions in which they worked.

In 1904, Marie's daughter Eve was born. This time too Pierre's father was a great help around the house and Marie could quickly resume her teaching work as well as her lab work, secure in the knowledge that the granddaughters were well looked after by their grandfather.

Pierre became Professor of Physics at the Sorbonne but by 1905 he realized he was not able to work for such long hours because of severe pain in his legs and hands.

In 1905 the Curies finally accepted their Nobel Prize for Physics and Pierre in his thank you speech warned of the dangers of radium and the destruction it could cause.

The very next year on a rainy day after an enjoyable lunch with some science professors, Pierre was walking down the streets to go to his publisher.

He quickly crossed the road without seeing the approaching wagon drawn by horses. He met with an accident in which his skull was crushed and he died instantly. Marie was heartbroken when she heard the news as she had also lost a companion with whom she had worked everyday. The funeral was a quiet one and as usual Marie kept aside personal grief and went back to work. She was soon offered her husband's post at the Sorbonne and she had the distinction of being the first woman professor at the Sorbonne.

Marie brought up her daughters on her won, ensuring they got good physical and intellectual development. She wanted her children to know more about science and chemistry. She even set up a school of her own. Her lab work continued and in recognition of her hard work she received the Nobel Prize for Chemistry in 1911 for her work on radium. Though this time she did go to receive the prize, her health was hardly in the best of conditions.

The work Marie had done on radioactivity paved the way for understanding the nature of the atom and nuclear physics.

After Pierre's death, Marie was romantically attached with fellow physicist Paul Langevin, who was a former pupil of her husband. Paul Langevin was unhappily married to a woman who lacked his educational achievements. He had four children and his wife felt he gave inadequate attention to the family. The affair finally came to an end after accusations against Curie by the French press of tarnishing the name of her deceased husband. The scandal finally blew over and the French academic world welcomed the first double Nobel laureate.

Marie's health meanwhile continued to get worse. She met Albert Einstein and shared a holiday with his family in the Alps. He admired her sparkling intellect and her discovery. They often discussed and wrote to each other about matters of science. Both feared that atomic power would be used in a war.

When the First World War broke out, the French government ordered her to hide the radium in her lab. They feared that the Germans would get hold of it. She deposited it in a bank vault in Bordeaux.

To help the wounded soldiers during the war, she specially designed a vehicle with X-Ray equipment, which became famous as the 'Little Curie'. Her daughter Irene also helped her mother raise money for equipment and teach and train women to use the X-Ray equipment.

The Pain Radium Institute was established in 1914. Marie became the Director in the year 1918.

Further research into radium revealed that some people were cured of their cancer by radium treatment.

In the year 1921, Marie and her two daughters sailed to U.S.A. where she was presented a casket of radium by President Warren Harding at the White House in Washington DC. This had all been originally initiated by an American journalist, Marie Meloney, who had interviewed Marie and was moved by her lack of funds.

Marie continued to travel and lecture extensively and raise funds for her Institute. She visited U.S.A. again in 1929 and was welcomed by President Herbert Hoover at the White House.

The harmful effects of radioactive substances started showing up when many scientists and X-Ray technicians suffered from anemia or lost their eyesight. Marie was also ill for many years by now. At the age of 66, Marie was diagnosed with the blood disease leukemia. She spent her last years in the Swiss mountains with her daughter Eve for company. The quiet end came on July 4, 1934.

Interestingly, Marie had two burials. On July 6, 1934 in the cemetery where her husband and in-laws lay buried in Sceaux and after 60 years her remains, along with those of her husband were reinterred in France's National Mausoleum in Paris, the Pantheon.

President Francois Mitterand had this to say of Marie Curie in his speech at the Pantheon in April, 1995:

"By transferring these ashes of Pierre and Marie Curie into the sanctuary of our collective memory, France not only performs an act of recognition, it also affirms a faith in science, in research, and its respect for those who dedicate themselves to science, just as Pierre and Marie Curie dedicated their energies and their lives to science."

The Radium Institute in Paris became an international center for the study of radioactivity. Till the time of Curie's death in the year 1934, the scientists there published a good number of 483 works. Besides Marie Curie published her own books and papers on research that she continued on polonium and actinium. She felt these elements should be scientifically observed and studied keeping in mind their practical applications in the field of medicine, science and industry.

She took it upon herself as a personal responsibility so that doctors and others, who used radium, could benefit by the services provided by the Institute.

So, more than her own research, she was interested in modernizing the Radium Institute. Of course, all of it to specialize about the one subject of her research and that was radioactivity.

Students who were trained at the Curie Institute constituted quite a few foreigners, including some women members, all of who were encouraged by Marie Curie's brisk but personal attention on a daily basis. In 1929, Solomon Rosenblum's work with actinium, that was prepared by Marie herself, confirmed the quantum theory, resulting in a major revelation. Irene, her daughter, and Frederic Joliot, her son-in-law, were actually involved in the research of her Institute. In the beginning of 1934, they were victorious in discovering artificial radioactivity, a discovery for which they would later win the Nobel Prize for Chemistry. That was in 1935 and sadly Irene's mother did not live long enough to witness that proud moment.

Marie's second daughter, Eve, though not science oriented as her sister, was talented in another field – writing. She even wrote a biography of her mother.

By strange coincidence, her granddaughter, Helene, eventually married Michel, who was the grandson of Paul Langevin, the same gentleman whom Marie could not get married to.

Even in her last years, Curie continued with her busy schedule and further involved herself in the Intellectual Co-operation of the League of Nations, to protect researcher's ownership of intellectual rights for their discoveries. Internationally, a bibliography of scientific papers was established, as also some work was done for scholarships in science.

That exposure to radiation and radioactivity can cause serious disease and ill effects on health, was still not clear to scientists of that day. In 1920, Marie's vision was severely impaired by a double cataract. She required four surgeries before she could resume her normal activity of writing and driving. The French Academy of Medicine recommended in 1925 that the workers in the lab use lead screens during the preparation of radioactive materials. Marie had attended the conference and saw to it that the staff at her Radium Institute underwent blood count checks on a regular basis. Regular exercise in open air was recommended.

It was beginning to dawn upon all that there could be some harmful effects also of radiation.

In a letter to Bronya, her sister, in November 1920, Marie Curie wrote: "Perhaps radium has something to do with these troubles but it cannot be affirmed with certainty."

Her own health was gradually deteriorating. She paid one last visit with her sister Bronya to meet her brother-in-law Jacques Curie. The doctors were unable to diagnose her illness. Later, after her death, the report of the sanatorium read: "The disease was an aplastic pernicious anemia of rapid, feverish development. The bone marrow did not react, probably because it had been injured by a long accumulation of radiation."

During the War, the French government requested the citizens to contribute their gold and silver and Curie thought it her duty to offer her two Nobel Medals and some others that were bestowed on her. Though the French National Bank turned down the offer, she used her prize money to buy war bonds. She even offered radiology courses to some American soldiers who were there in France at that time.

"The story of radiology in war offers a striking example of the unsuspected amplitude that the application of purely scientific discoveries can take under certain conditions. X-Rays had only a limited usefulness up to the time of war.....a similar evolution took place in radium therapy, the medical applications of radiations emitted by the radio elements." – *excerpt from the book 'Radiology in War'*.

The field of medicine has benefited from Marie's discovery, especially for cancer treatment. Millions and millions people across the globe have been treated by radiotherapy. The Paris Radium Institute continues its research department. The medical division has treated over 6000 people.

Marie Curie, the famous woman scientist who gave us this invaluable invention, had essentially worked with two motivating ideals in her life. The first was to do something of service to humanity at large and the second, to honour the memory of her husband Pierre.

What better way to conclude than to quote what Albert Einstein, the great physicist, had to say of her:

"Marie Curie is, of all celebrated beings, the one whose fame is not corrupted."

⌘ ❖ ⌘